Finding England

Finding England

An Ausländer's Guide to Perfidious Albion

by
Holger Ehling

Armchair Traveller
at the bookHaus

First published in the UK in 2012 by
The Armchair Traveller *at the bookHaus*
The bookHaus, 70 Cadogan Place, London SW1X 9AH
www.thearmchairtraveller.com

ISBN 978 1 907973 24 6
ebook ISBN 978 1 907973 26 0

Typeset in Garamond by MacGuru Ltd
info@macguru.org.uk

Printed and bound in China by 1010 Printing International Ltd

A CIP catalogue for this book is available from the British Library

For John and Paul

Contents

Welcome

This royal throne of kings, this sceptred isle,
This earth of majesty, this seat of Mars,
This other Eden, demi-paradise,
This fortress built by Nature for herself
Against infection and the hand of war,
This happy breed of men, this little world,
This precious stone set in the silver sea,
Which serves it in the office of a wall
Or as a moat defensive to a house,
Against the envy of less happier lands,
This blessed plot, this earth, this realm, this England.

William Shakespeare, *Richard II*, Act 2, Scene 1

When I came to England for the first time, at the tender age of thirteen, it was to improve my English. Many people do this; according to the British Council, more than one billion people worldwide are learning English. That's pretty impressive. And even though England and the United Kingdom have long been outdone by the United States in terms of economic prowess and pop-cultural allure, King

Richard's 'Sceptred Isle' still reigns supreme when it comes to the prestigious end of the language-teaching market.

But why do people come to study, why do they come to visit, why do they come to stay? England's attractiveness to visitors certainly has little to do with the weather or with its culinary offerings. 'When you walk through the storm / hold your head up high...' – these first lines of 'You'll Never Walk Alone', the iconic hymn from *Carousel*, seem to capture most foreigners' ideas about England. Rain and wind come to mind first. And awful food, of course – it's nice to have stereotypes. Just as in: all Americans are fat and stupid. All French people lust for frogs' legs and covet their neighbours' wives. All Germans wear *Lederhosen* and eat sauerkraut all the time.

This does not sound too promising, does it? I, being German, haven't worn *Lederhosen* since I was three years old. But I do love my sauerkraut.

But how should one describe the English? If you are trying to describe a whole nation, stereotypes can help but even though they may have a shadow of truth about them, they never work for the individual. It's probably best to go back to Shakespeare; this time it is Shylock's famous plea:

> If you tickle us, do we not laugh? If you poison us, do we not die? And if you wrong us, shall we not revenge? If we are like you in the rest, we will resemble you in that.

William Shakespeare, *The Merchant of Venice*, Act 3, Scene 1

Let us adhere to the spirit of Shylock's plea and assume that the English are basically as human as the rest of us.

That said, here goes our list of stereotypes, and you are welcome to add to these: The English are always polite. The English are a bunch of violent hooligans. The English are unshakeable and unexcitable, they are reluctant to show their emotions and always keep a 'stiff upper lip'. The English are eccentrics. The English regard their home as their castle. The English cannot cook. The English love to drink (a lot), whatever it may be – tea, beer, you name it. The English have fantastically large ears (think of Prince Charles) and very bad teeth. The English have a questionable sense of personal hygiene (an Australian swimming coach once applauded the success of England's swimmers saying it wasn't bad 'for a nation that has very few swimming pools and not much soap,'). The English have a sense of humour. The English are impeccably dressed. English girls and women never wear stockings, even in winter. English men go bare-chested at the slightest hint of sunshine. The English are charitable and tolerant. The English hate foreigners and they don't speak foreign languages.

What do we make of this? You will have noted that there are quite a number of contradictions in this list of stereotypes. For the sake of fun, we will explore some of them in this book and see how far we get.

Our list of stereotypes implies that we 'aliens' seem to know England very well. It may have to do with the fact that most of us had to learn English at school and so tended to pick up some ideas about the country's geography and its people's behaviour from an early age. And don't forget that we too have our home-grown versions of *Hello* or *OK!* which bring us all sorts of tittle-tattle originating from England's royalty – both the Windsor and the Posh & Becks varieties. Many of us aliens seem to know more about the shenanigans of the House of Windsor than about our own extended family. Television also helps, with its hundreds of English series, from *Upstairs, Downstairs* to *Downton Abbey*, from *Morse* to *Midsomer Murders*, painting a very specific image of England. Given that most of these series are crime programmes, one gets the impression that England is a rather dangerous place.

Well, it isn't.

We all have 'English' images in our heads: the Queen, the Yorkshire Dales or the Channel coast, the red buses and the black cabs, the charming local pubs and the lovely village greens. These are images of an idealised England and many of them centre on the idea, or rather the *ideal* of the English countryside, which has been the imaginary Eden for the English soul for hundreds of years, acting as a counterfoil to the deprivations of city life. We are talking about a country that was the first in Europe to develop massive urban settlements. For a long time, the idea of 'the country' has been idolised by city-dwellers who yearn for this Eden, whilst huddled up on their cosy couches in Islington or Chelsea, or Hamburg,

Pittsburgh or Madrid for that matter – the English country-side has become an international myth; a myth that has more to do with Bucolic ideals than with reality.

Of course, living in the city means that you don't actually have to go to the country, and thus you avoid the mud and the damp, and the lack of proper public transport, a drink-able caffè latte and most of the civic services that you rely on in your everyday urban life. But it is nice to know that some-where out there, this kind of Eden exists.

Country living has also become a fashion statement: the Barbour jacket has become *de rigueur* among the smart urban set all over the world (I confess that I own one myself), and wearing a tweed sports jacket to work has become quite common, outside Britain at least. And of course, city-dwellers have adopted country car choices too; you just have to have that SUV to face the perils of the daily school run or to brave the risks of your 30-minute drive to the office.

But behind these seemingly familiar images lurks an England that remains foreign because when we travel to England, we tend to stay in London, which is as representative of England as New York is of the USA. Meaning, not. We tend to hear a lot about the Royals and politics and the economy and football – but hardly ever do we get reports about every-day life in England, about what it is like to live in a country that is still class-ridden, in a society that proclaims itself as being multicultural and inclusive but which tends to organise itself along ethnic lines.

Apart from trying to find out what 'the English' are like, in this book we will try to look behind the obvious and find out about England's history, its culture and its everyday life. We will travel around the country (but be warned: this is *not* a book of travel writing and it is *not* a travel guide) as well as spending a lot of time in London. When we leave the big city we will go to a lot of different places, from Hadrian's Wall in the north to Stonehenge in the south, to the Eden Project in Cornwall and to the marvels of Blackpool, pondering along the way what it is that makes these places 'English'. We will meet royals and beggars, con-artists and real artists, heroes and villains, English roses, plumbers and the legacy of the Empire. We will talk about the arts, sports, about the weather and, of course, about the food.

History is important; just look around in any city in England; the complex history of each place is evident wherever you go. There are not that many countries in the world where you can see so many people of so many different ethnicities. Without England's imperial past – it once called a quarter of the globe its own – this would not be the case.

I have already said that stereotypes can be quite useful. Even though I don't wear *Lederhosen*, I feel distinctly German. What's true for me is certainly true for England and the English. There is bad weather. Lots of bad weather, actually, if you're in the wrong place at the wrong time. But my memories of England in fog and rain are surpassed by my memories of glorious spring days with crisp air, blue skies and a light that is unlike anywhere else. Idling the time away on a Sunday afternoon in a country pub, John Major comes to mind (well, to my mind). This hapless former Prime Minister, successor to Margaret Thatcher, has more or less vanished from public memory in England, except for one quote that will forever be used to describe his 'little Englander' vision of the country. In a speech to his Conservative Party in 1993 he said:

> Fifty years on from now, Britain will still be the country of long shadows on cricket grounds, warm beer, invincible green suburbs, dog lovers and pools fillers and, as George Orwell said, 'Old maids bicycling to holy communion through the morning mist' and, if we get our way, Shakespeare will still be read even in school.*

It was not only Major's breathtakingly backward-looking view that confused audiences then and still confuses us today, but also his complete disregard for the impetus of George Orwell's essay 'The Lion and the Unicorn', from which he quotes. Orwell's piece was a scathing attack on the political system and the intellectual and political classes of his time – and much of it still rings true today. In fact, Orwell's ideas are

---

* Speech to the Conservative Group for Europe, 22 April 1993. The reference to George Orwell is to his 1941 essay 'The Lion and the Unicorn'.

diametrically opposed to those of the Prime Minister who came not only to misunderstand and misquote Orwell, but also to misrepresent him. John Major makes it sound as if paradise was a place at the end of the yellow brick road, a Noddy-land, only with rhyming couplets.

Even the England I got to know some forty years ago had nothing to do with Major's idealised vision. Most English people do not live in thatched cottages in quaint little villages but have to make do with overpriced accommodation in urban areas. England is not a laid-back nation of old maids cycling to Holy Communion. It is vibrant and cosmopolitan and has been tremendously enriched by the multiculturalism of the post-war years. It has even – shock! horror! – become a European country, despite what the English may say. Who would have thought forty years ago that England would become a gourmet's paradise? Well, if you can afford it.

You may not see too many gentlemen wearing bowler hats in the City today, the fabulous red double-decker Routemaster buses have been replaced by faceless modern machines, and even the dreaded fogs in London are a thing of the past. But there are still remnants of quaint old England: the Morris dancing and the Mob Football, the garden parties and Royal Ascot, Swan-Upping and Cheese-Rolling and the Boat Race, and, of course, the wonderful, rolling green hills and open spaces that you can marvel at, once you have left the big city.

My first visit to England was to be the first of many and I

have spent some of my happiest years in Her Majesty's realm. I hope, dear reader, that my little book will convey some of my fondness for the country and its people and that you too will be fascinated by this wonderful part of the world, 'This blessed plot, this earth, this realm, this England.'

Frankfurt and London
April 2012

Finding England. England?

It is easy to find England on a map – it is part of that large thing in the North Sea, just off the French coast and a bit to the left of Denmark and Norway. It gets trickier once you are there; not even the English are keen or even able to explain what *England* actually is.

Well, first of all, it is not Great Britain, although even within her Majesty's realm, people sometimes overlook this distinction. There are actually six names which are quite often used without much thought to describe it: apart from England, you will hear people talk about 'Britain', 'Great Britain', the 'United Kingdom', the 'British Isles' and – when pomp and circumstance demand – 'Albion'.

But in this book, we will not deal with the array of Celtic neighbours – when we speak about England, we speak about the eastern part of the southern half of the island. Especially for foreigners, it is sound advice not to suggest that everyone living in Britain is somehow English – the Scots in particular tend to dislike the idea, and if you happen to stumble upon a

Welshman, you are in grave danger of causing him to break out in song or say something in his own language, which you won't understand and which might leave you reaching for a towel. The Irish will be split in their reactions: Protestant Unionists might correct you but not take too much offence, Catholic Republicans might, at best, douse you with a Guinness.

In case you find such remarks slightly offensive – don't worry, the English themselves give as good as they get. A couple of years ago Anne Robinson, the dominatrix of UK television as hostess of *The Weakest Link*, asked 'What are the Welsh for?' – and, of course, nobody could come up with an answer. And if somebody should really take offence, there's always the reference to the common sense of humour.

The English tend to think of themselves as superior to their Celtic neighbours: the Irish are characterised as a bunch of chaotic and rebellious drunkards; the Scots are honest but dull, or 'dour' – P.G. Wodehouse once said 'It is never difficult to distinguish between a Scotsman with a grievance and a ray of sunshine.' Think of Gordon Brown, Tony Blair's hapless (Scottish) successor as Prime Minister, and you have to admit there might really be some truth in Wodehouse's suggestion. And as for the Welsh – well, you just heard about them.

So, once again – this book is about England and the English. Let us begin with the basics: England is not a very big place. With Scotland to the north and Wales to the west, England occupies roughly 130,000 square kilometres, which is about the size of Alabama, or a third of the size of Germany. France is five times as big as England. The distances are manageable: from London to Newcastle in the north east, or from London to St. Ives in Cornwall, it is about 450 kilometres, about the same distance as between Amsterdam and Frankfurt. But this compact area is home to some 50 million people, out of a total of about 60 million living in the United Kingdom. Especially in London and the south east, space is at a premium.

London is, of course, the major urban area, with just over 7 million inhabitants; within the M25 circle there are about 11 million people. The second largest English city, Birmingham, just scrambles past the one million mark, and Sheffield, the third largest city, has just over 500,000 inhabitants. Given this huge agglomeration of people (and jobs and businesses), it is understandable that most Londoners are in doubt whether there is life as we know it beyond Oxford.

When it comes to administration, England happily preserves the structures introduced in Norman times, a bit like their French neighbours on the other side of the Channel. Where the French have their *départements*, the English have their counties, most of which are called something '-shire', which is sometimes pronounced as in 'wire' and at other times as in 'fur'. There is no way of knowing which pronunciation is correct – just speak as you think it should be done and wait for the reaction. Whereas in federal states, such as the USA or Germany, you have large provinces or states with devolved governments, traditionally there was no such administrative or legislative layer between local and central government in the United Kingdom, which led to a rather high degree of dependence upon the Powers That Be in London.

One of the early projects of the Labour government that came to power in 1997 was to introduce devolved parliaments in Scotland, Wales and Northern Ireland. This was a nice gesture on the one hand, but it also brought about a strengthening of the nationalist parties: Plaid Cymru in Wales and the Scottish Nationalists saw to it that Labour did not have too much fun with the new institutions. At the time of writing, the Scottish Nationalist government was preparing a referendum on the dissolution of the union with England – we will see how this pans out.

Scotland, Wales and Northern Ireland all eventually received their devolved parliaments – England didn't. Nobody (and certainly no one in the former Labour government that brought devolution about) has been able to give a reason. Someone ventured, in lieu of a real explanation, that England was too large and populous for its own devolved parliament. (Now just fancy suggesting this to any self-regarding Texan, Catalan or Bavarian...) Instead of a devolved parliament, England got eight unelected regional assemblies, which were stuffed with worthies and party cronies who needed to make a little bit of money without too much of an obligation.

Behind this rather bizarre political flummery is the 'West Lothian question' – the fundamental question about who is allowed to legislate about what. Scottish or Welsh members of the national parliament in Westminster are allowed to vote when it comes to legislation that only affects England – English MPs have no say over much of the legislation pertaining to their Celtic neighbours. When Labour introduced plans for the privatisation of hospitals and new fees for university students in England, they had to muster all their Scottish and Welsh MPs to get the legislation through the House – a piece of legislation that had been dismissed by the devolved parliaments, meaning that only the English had to suffer the consequences.

In everyday life, most English, Scots, Welsh and Irish regard themselves as of different nationalities within the 'United Kingdom of Great Britain and Northern Ireland'; being 'British' plays second fiddle. This manifests itself in the tradition of having separate national teams in soccer, rugby and cricket (where the English and Welsh join forces). Their rivals don't mind: international successes for these teams are rare occurrences. (Well, the English cricketers are doing alright at the moment – but just give it some time, they'll sink back into oblivion soon enough.) Conversely, in the sports where there are united British teams, such as athletics or swimming or cycling, these teams tend to perform successfully.

Back to the administrative structure of the country: there are now 40 counties in England, plus six Metropolitan Areas, plus 81 larger administrative units. But of course, there is also a gaggle of 'Ceremonial Counties', 'Registration Counties', 'Historic Counties' and, last but not least, the 'Former Postal

Counties'. They all have retained some meaning and importance to this day – but hardly anyone is sure of the details.

Many of today's counties go back to Anglo-Saxon and Norman times. Since the seventh century, the various kings rewarded their most loyal followers with the run of some stretches of land; the shires. The rewardee was allowed to call himself 'Count', the shire became a county. Today, a Count normally calls himself 'Earl', although his wife remains a 'Countess'.

England became England long before most other countries in Europe became unified. King Æthelstan unified the dominant Anglo-Saxon kingdoms of his day in AD 927. The Venerable Bede, the most important historian of Anglo-Saxon England, used the term 'Anglefolk' in the eighth century, which only went to show that the nation had been taken over by Germans; Angles, Saxons and Jutes (who had arrived in the fifth century) were of solid Northern German stock.

Other things you may find interesting:

Out of the 50 million inhabitants of England, 90 per cent are of European origin; 5.3 per cent hail from South Asia (India, Pakistan, Bangladesh, Sri Lanka); 2.7 per cent are of African or West Indian origin.

Economically, England is the powerhouse of Great Britain; according to the OECD, its GDP in 2007 was $2800 billion (USD), which is approximately $45,000 (USD) per capita. If London were a country, its economic power would put it on par with countries such as Austria. London is also the EU's largest and most populous metropolitan area.

15

England was the first European country to introduce a semblance of a parliament; the English judicial system is regarded as a model around the globe. In many former colonies, the English Law Lords are accepted as the highest judicial authority.

The Royal Society was the world's first scientific association, leading to tremendous advances in research and development, and laying the foundations for the industrial revolution.

England was the first European country to grant Freedom of the Press (1695) and to pass a Copyright Act (1710) which acknowledged the intellectual property rights of artists and writers.

And of course, England ruled the largest colonial empire in the world's history. At the beginning of the twentieth century, a quarter of the planet was part of it. Today, memories of colonial grandeur and images of English ladies being carried atop Indian elephants tend to push aside the historical truth. England played a major part in the slave trade, in the plundering of natural resources across five continents, in the systematic killing of indigenous people in the Americas and Australia – to name just a few of many not very telegenic truths. Queen Elizabeth I personally profited from the slave trade; Queen Victoria, in authorising the Opium War against China, became one of the most ruthless drug dealers in the world's history. Such things would not have a place in your average Merchant Ivory movie. Regrets about this tarnished past are seldom expressed by the English, and if some politician does express remorse, it is often delivered with the kind of sincerity that one would expect from a bunch of boys who have kicked their football through a window and now have to apologise in order to appease their parents.

Westminster, London

Where we find bongs and gongs; explosive taxes;
honours, cash and an Iron Lady

Bing-bong-bing-bong... yes, we all know Big Ben or rather, 'The Clock Tower at the Palace of Westminster', as it is officially known. 'The Sound of England' rings out every hour. At the time of writing, an effort was under way to rename it 'Elizabeth Tower' to honour the 60th anniversary of the monarch's coronation, but even the proponents of the renaming admitted that Her Majesty's name probably would not replace 'Big Ben' in popular usage. English humour may be to blame for putting one of the most loved English buildings in the same spot as some of its most loathed people – the members of the two Houses of Parliament.

I thought it would be a fitting start to our journey in search of England and the English to go to the political heart of the nation's capital – most foreigners will start their visits there too. There is much to be seen, from the skyscraping elegance of Westminster Abbey, to the architectural mediocrity that is Buckingham Palace; the beautiful parks and the government buildings you find in Whitehall. The area was once far away from the old city of London; it was in the mid-eleventh century that building works started for an abbey and an adjoining palace. Only since the sixteenth century has there been a conjunction between Westminster and the rest of London; keeping itself to itself is still something that Westminster is very good at.

But we have wandered away from Big Ben, which is actually not the tower but the large bell that rings out the deepest of the hourly 'bongs'. The bell itself is named after either a famed prize boxer or the man in charge of the rebuilding of the palace.

Rebuilding the palace?

Yes, the huge construction overlooking the Thames may look ancient, but it is actually quite modern. The rebuilding became necessary after a fire destroyed the old palace in 1834, and of course, the tax office was to blame: parliament had at long last decided to burn the wooden 'tally sticks', some of them dating back to Anglo-Saxon times, which had been used as evidence of payments received from taxpayers. Charles Dickens pleaded with the authorities to hand these sticks out to the poor as fuel in winter time, but the sticks were declared official documents, which had to be destroyed officially. Well, they were destroyed in a very official way – burning like tinder, the centuries-old wood overheated the boilers underneath the old Palace of Westminster, which did what overheated boilers tend to do: they exploded. The resulting fire reduced the grandiose old palace to a heap of rubble. (Oh, one more thing you may wish to know about Her Majesty's tax people: they still have not managed to bring the tax year in line with the calendar year, following the switch from the Julian to the Gregorian calendar in 1752. Which is why the tax year in this country starts on 6th April.)

But we mustn't stray. When it came to the decision over the style in which to rebuild the palace, the building commission decided to shun modern, functional architecture and opted for the mock-gothic style that was all the rage at the time.

The old palace had been used by parliament since the sixteenth century. The replacement took almost thirty years to complete; it incorporates what was left of the old building, but it is much bigger. The frontage on the Thames measures 266 metres; the site covers more than three hectares and contains more than 1,100 rooms, the most important of which are, of course, the two chambers of parliament.

Impressive as the building is, what happens inside is even more important. Both the House of Commons and the House of Lords operate on centuries of tradition. The balance between the two chambers is that of a finely tuned instrument, and it has served the country well. The House of Commons with its elected members is the main legislative institution, but the House of Lords, whose members are either appointed or hereditary, has every right to alter, send back and, in some cases, even reject a bill.

The House of Commons is elected in a first-past-the-post system, which means that small parties stand little chance of forming a power base in parliament. This has led to a long tradition of two main parties alternating in government; only the Liberal Democrats (Lib Dems) have attained a significant presence as a third party and in 2010, they became part of the first coalition government since the Second World War. Sometimes the majority of a ruling party may be huge in terms of seats in parliament but only small in terms of the overall number of votes won. The smaller parties have cried foul over this arrangement for a long time and have demanded the introduction of proportional representation. Fat chance – why would the Tories and Labour want to change a system that has served them so well for so long?

On a positive note, the first-past-the-post system has kept out many undesirable elements; when fascist and communist parties were blossoming in Europe in the 1930s, the fascist movement in England never got into parliament. George Orwell once remarked that the monarchy may be the best safeguard against political extremism, but it seems the electoral system itself is a pretty solid defence. When you look at the results of the latest elections for the European Parliament in 2009, which is held under proportional representation, it shows that the political landscape in Britain is much more factious than the Westminster system implies: the 'victorious' Tories got 28 per cent, the right-wing UK Independence Party (UKIP) got 17 per cent, followed by Labour with 16 per cent, the LibDems with 14 per cent, the Green Party with 9 per cent and the British National Party, (which, being aware of the English libel laws, I would not dream of calling neo-fascist,) with 6 per cent.*

An irrefutable argument for the existing system is the direct responsibility of the MPs to their constituents. If they fail to hold clinics in their constituencies on a regular basis or if they ignore local problems, re-selection by their local party will be difficult. From time to time, the system also allows for independent candidates campaigning on single-issue platforms of local importance to beat the candidates of the big parties. Their influence in parliament is nil, but their election brings the issue to the attention of the big parties, and quite often the debated problem will be resolved.

The close contact most MPs have with their constituents does not mean that politicians are more popular in England than they are in other countries. Public opinion sees them as mendacious grabbers who only have their own advantage in mind. When the big expenses scandal broke in 2009, revealing that many members of both Houses had abused the system that reimbursed them for maintaining homes in their constituencies, these negative sentiments were confirmed. It simply does not look good if a minister is found to have claimed expenses on the subscription to a porn channel, or if one MP claims expenses for having the moat of his castle cleaned and another for sprucing up his duck pond. With ducks in play, one is not surprised that lots of eggs ended up on lots of faces,

---

* 'European Election 2009: UK Results'. *BBC News*, 8 June 2009.

and many political careers ended unceremoniously and in deep ignominy.

To us foreigners, much of what goes on in the two chambers of the British parliament looks like a protracted effort at making things as incomprehensible as possible. The seating arrangement with government and opposition facing each other across the floor lends itself to a confrontational style of argument. And in fact, much of what you hear, especially during Prime Minister's Questions, is only designed to grab headlines. Shouting and waving papers at your opponent seems to be mandatory and passions are not really tempered by the odd rule that you cannot call another member of the House by his or her name. So you are not allowed to say that John Doe MP, is an idiot; instead you have to phrase it 'The Honourable Member for Fiddlesticks is off his rocker.' Members of both chambers are also not allowed to say the name of the other chamber; instead it has to be 'this place' and 'another place'.

Whatever you may think of the quality of the debates in both chambers, you cannot beat them when it comes to ceremony. Think of the annual opening performed by the Queen herself: the lords in ermine robes, 'Black Rod' as master of ceremonies dressed in medieval costume. Sadly, since 1313 nobody has been allowed to wear shining armour in parliament – it would certainly not be inappropriate for this ceremony, which is right up there with some of the more outlandish rituals you see performed in ancient Hollywood movies about India or Africa.

Where the House of Commons exudes an air of bickering and posturing, the House of Lords resembles an oasis of calm. This may have to do with the fact that many of its members are quite elderly and seem to enjoy having a warm place to stretch out their creaking limbs. Traditionally, the House of Lords was made up of hereditary peers and a couple of bishops from the Church of England. This assured a fierce independence of the House, which any true-blooded government will of course regard as obstinacy. The first attempts at major reforms were announced during Victoria's reign, and again in 1911, but all to no avail.

In 1958, the 'Life Peerage' was introduced which allowed the parties to get political activists into the upper chamber. It was an easy way to get rid of politicians who had blotted their copybook through scandal or disobedience or who had simply reached their sell-by date in terms of age. And it was a good way for the parties to make a little money on the side: cash for honours is of course illegal, but a sizeable donation never impeded a person's chance to see their name mentioned in the Honours List. During Tony Blair's tenure as Prime Minister, his offices were searched by police who were investigating such deals, and New Labour had to repay loans it had received from wealthy 'friends'. As the affair had to do with 'honours', one might have thought that a person would have resigned from office after such an embarrassment, but such thoughts were never a problem for Blair. Eventually he pushed through some reforms: all but 92 hereditary peers had to leave the Lords and a commission was installed to oversee the appointment of new ones. In theory, everyone is eligible; in practice, the system strengthened the steady flow of party faithfuls into the chamber. At the time of writing, efforts were under way to turn the House of Lords into a fully-elected chamber; the public reactions were furious, to put it mildly.

You, dear reader, can become a Lord quite easily, too, if you are willing to fork out around £2,000 – that will buy you the title of 'Lord of the Manor'. Just look it up on the internet.

The English system, with its two big political parties handing over power to each other from time to time, does not normally create violent ideological swings. From the Second World War onwards, the Tories and Labour had a consensus on the major issues, and the government administration with its powerful civil servants tended to make sure that the transitions went smoothly.

And then there was Margaret Thatcher.

When *The Iron Lady,* the film starring Merryl Streep, premiered in England in early 2012, the reaction was split, as it always is when it comes to Thatcher and her legacy – half the people thought that the scenes in which she was shown as a frail old lady ravaged by dementia lacked respect; the other half thought that the depiction of her persona was too sympathetic. Whatever your personal opinion of Thatcher may be, you will always find somebody in England who will oppose you vehemently.

All this goes to show that today's political village in Westminster, and indeed, the whole country, is still in awe of the Iron Lady. Her legacy is a nation that is more deeply divided along social and racial lines than at any time since the Second World War; some would say that the thirteen years of Labour government between 1997 and 2010 have even entrenched these divisions. No other leading industrial nation in Europe has so many children living in poverty; estimated at four million, or 30 per cent. Every fifth household in the United Kingdom depends totally on social benefits. Liverpool, once the thriving capital of industry and trading, is the worst off: 32 per cent of households do not have a single member with a job. Non-white people living in England go to prison five times more often than whites; black university graduates earn 24 per cent less than their white compatriots.

This is Margaret Thatcher's legacy. Let's talk about her.

Margaret Thatcher was born in 1925 in Grantham, the Lincolnshire town where Isaac Newton received his education. Just like Newton, she had a knack for sciences – she studied chemistry at Oxford and was part of the team that invented Soft Ice. Her father was a grocer and Methodist preacher; this may well have shaped her belief that everyone is responsible only to himself. Having married a rich oil trader, she went back to university and became a barrister. From 1959 until 1992 she was the MP for Finchley and made a name for herself in the early 1960s through her campaign to re-introduce caning in schools. This duly qualified her for her first senior post in government: she became Secretary of State for Education and Science. In office, she made waves by scrapping the supply of free milk to school children, earning her the moniker 'Maggie Thatcher, Milk Snatcher'. In 1975 she became leader of the Conservative Party.

When Thatcher won the general election in 1979, she took over a country that had gone through years of economic downturn and a turbulent winter, during which various strike actions had left garbage uncollected, patients untreated and the dead unburied (yes, the gravediggers went on strike too). She turned to the job ruthlessly, destroying trade unions, privatising nationalised industries and shutting down uneconomical collieries, steel plants and shipping yards. Her way of doing things was highly unpopular, even within her own party, and she looked certain to lose the next elections when the Argentine military junta threw her a lifeline by invading that preposterous remnant of English colonialism, the Falkland Islands, in 1982. The nation rallied around their leader, who retook the islands, assured re-election and stayed in power for a total of eleven and a half years.

Thatcher's reforms destroyed the post-war consensus between the parties, which had been based on the principle that business and the state were there to serve the population. In Thatcher's world, the state and population were there to serve business – and it has remained like this ever since. The most devastating effects of her reforms were felt in the former industrial heartlands in the north of England. Cities like Manchester, Liverpool or Newcastle became economic disaster zones, because the destruction of the old industries was not accompanied by efficient measures to create new ones.

Within a month of coming to power, Thatcher unshackled the financial markets, abolishing all capital controls, making it legal to transfer any amount of money out of the country without it being taxed. Bona fide tax black holes such as Panama or the Cayman Islands prospered; corporate and private tax avoidance became common – thanks to Thatcher, the super rich became even richer, while the great unwashed had their benefits slashed. To this day, the present Prime Minister David Cameron and his family allegedly profit from such tax dodging schemes – we can be sure that he will do his utmost to end these practices, can't we?

Greed became the ethos of Thatcher's days: telecommunications, water, energy supply and many more of the national infrastructure services were privatised, creating fantastic opportunities for getting rich quick by upping prices and lowering standards. Rail privatisation, which was finalised during the tenure of John Major, is a striking example: the private rail industry today receives about four times as much in subsidies as during the days of nationalised rail, while providing fewer trains and connections.

Yes, Thatcher was right to scrap the top rate of income tax, which in a few cases reached 98 per cent; she was right to curb the influence of the trade unions, which had paralysed the economy; she was right to get rid of ridiculous state interference, even in small things like setting the price of a haircut. But she also caused a massive real estate bubble by forcing councils to sell their housing stock to tenants at vastly reduced prices. This led to a drastic shortage of affordable housing and the pushing aside of the poorest sections of the population. The middle and upper classes, traditional Tory clientele, profited immensely, but 25 per cent of the population found themselves living below the poverty line.

Thatcher did not do mercy; her most famous description of her concept of society shows her utter contempt for it:

> There is no such thing as society. There are individual men
> and women, and there are families. And no government
> can do anything except through people, and people
> must look to themselves first. It's our duty to look after
> ourselves and then, also to look after our neighbour.
> People have got the entitlements too much in mind,
> without the obligation.*

When the Tories eventually lost power in 1997, it became clear very quickly that the 'New' Labour government was not going to change many of the Thatcherite policies. Social benefits continued to be cut year after year; services such as prison management or setting school exams continued to be privatised; unruly youths were now threatened with ASBOs

---

* Interview, 23 September 1987. *Woman's Own*, 31.10.1987: 8–10.

(Anti-Social Behaviour Orders), which led to the late come-dienne Linda Smith's quip, '...you have to bear in mind they are the only qualification some of these kids are going to get.'

During the thirteen years of Labour government, the involvement of the private sector became even more important than it had been before: trying to keep expensive infrastructure investments off the public balance sheets, Public-Private Partnerships and Private Finance Initiatives were used to build hospitals, roads or schools. This has created a monstrous shadow debt book which will haunt state finances for decades to come.

The present Tory-Lib Dem coalition – the first coalition government since the Second World War – is struggling to come to terms with the effects of the off-balance legacies, as well as those of the burst real estate bubble and the resulting financial crisis. And they have taken the opportunity to cut spending even further, creating an even wider gap between the haves and the have-nots. To soften the blow, they have come up with the idea of a 'Big Society', which is supposed 'to create a climate that empowers local people and communities.' It basically means that government reduces its social involvement even more, handing over the responsibility of care for those who are in need to private initiative and charity. This must be what Thatcher had in mind when she said that 'there is no such thing as society.'

Chipping Norton, Oxfordshire

Where we meet toffs, mockneys, Professor Higgins
and no rain in Spain

Oh, the upper classes of England. In so many newspaper articles we are told that England remains the most class-ridden country in Europe – if you haven't known the right people from the very start, it is difficult to get to the top. And even then, we are told, you will forever remain the upstart, the alien, the *parvenu*. Well, this may be the case but in recent times we have learned that there is hope for almost anybody to rub shoulders with the high and mighty; as long as you have made some dough, that is. And nowhere is this as true as in Chipping Norton, the lovely market town in Oxfordshire. There are remnants of an old castle, some medieval buildings and a clutter of Georgian houses around the market, much as you would expect to see in this part of the country, which had always thrived on the wool trade. Nearby is Blenheim Castle with its magnificent park, and a plethora of quaint villages and lovely cottages. It has attracted the well-to-do for many years.

But Chipping Norton's recent claim to fame is due to the fact that it is part of Witney, the constituency of Prime Minister David Cameron, who has invested in a nice country pile to be closer to both his constituents and the smart set he likes to hang out with. So, the good people of Oxfordshire are regularly treated to the spectacle of politicos and aristocrats, actors and media types hitting the bubbly and donning their Barbours. A newspaper recently quoted a local saying 'Every weekend there are drinks parties, barbecues, swimming and tennis parties. And in the winter there's shooting and hunting. There's a great mix of people, though it's pretty high octane.'*

'High octane' is an apt description for the Chipping Norton set, who would of course tell you that there is nothing elite about them. Just because you once ran the biggest tabloid rags in the country before being arrested by the police (Rebekah Brooks) or because you still run the most influential PR firm (Mathew Freud); you are the daughter of the world's leading media magnate (Elisabeth Murdoch, married to Freud) or a rock star (Alex James of Blur), a TV car show presenter (Jeremy Clarkson), a super model (Kate Moss), or you just own lots of stuff (the Bamford family of JCB digger fame; Charlie Dunstone of Carphone Warehouse; Emily Oppenheimer Turner of DeBeers), doesn't mean you're not completely down to earth, does it? And it certainly does not call for comments such as the one by the *Daily Telegraph*'s Peter Oborne who called it 'an incestuous collection of louche, affluent, power-hungry and

---

* James Hanning/Matthew Bell: 'Rebekah, Dave, and the Chipping Norton set: Where power in Britain lies'. *Independent on Sunday*, 10 July 2011.

amoral Londoners, located in and around the Prime Minister's Oxfordshire constituency.'* Shocking, isn't it?

Well, some are more equal than others, and it is all very democratic: everybody is allowed his say, but in the end, things are done to suit the needs of the establishment of the day.

In the 1970s, *Upstairs, Downstairs* was a popular TV series (it was revived in 2011) which portrayed life in a posh house in London's Belgravia. The daily troubles and joys of the rich family who owned the house were contrasted with those of their loyal servants, who dwelt in the basement. The psychological distance between the classes contrasted with their physical proximity, and the impossibility of forming genuine bonds across the class divide was painfully visible throughout.

Historically, class distinctions became part of the national psyche when the Normans invaded England: the new masters saw to it that their underlings were firmly kept in place. This is still manifest in the English language, just look at the different words used to name animals and the meals their meat provides: cow and beef, pig and pork, stag and venison, and so on. The English-speaking underlings reared the animals, the French-speaking upper class dined on them.

In the 'good old days', any proper working-class family had the ambition to 'better' their life and get into the middle class.

---

* Peter Oborne: 'David Cameron is in the sewer because of his News International friends.' *Daily Telegraph*, 6 July 2011.

A house with a garden and a car in front of it was the ultimate proof of having made it. Language was another sign of class: the key to success was clear and proper English and anybody with an ambition to be upwardly mobile binned his regional accent.

Today, this has changed completely: hardly anyone who wishes to remain popular with the media-consuming public will admit to having been born middle class; without a rags-to-riches-story, you are just not the juicy bit of fodder the tabloids want. Proper English is regarded as snobbery; if you want to get anywhere, you have to sport some kind of regional accent. Tony Blair attracted scorn and derision when he, who had grown up in Edinburgh, Adelaide and Durham, started to fake a Cockney accent and 'drop his aitches' on breakfast television.

Even the BBC, which we foreigners regard as the stand-ard bearer for good English, has flooded its programmes with people who do not speak with the old Received Pronun-ciation, but instead sport broad Scouse (Liverpool), Geordie (Newcastle) or Scottish accents. 'Why can't the English teach their children how to speak?' is what Professor Higgins asks in *My Fair Lady*, adding that the French don't care what you do as long as you pronounce it properly. Wise words.

The working class has become part of urban folklore; this is where the heart of England beats, these people are 'the salt of the earth'. Even the old urban low-life gets a glorified review, such as the Kray twins, who headed one of the most violent gangs in London's East End during the 1960s. Go to any old boozer round the Mile End Road and you are likely to hear that 'they were always well-behaved, you know'.

The educational reforms after the Second World War provided new opportunities to the working classes. Comprehensive schools and new universities helped to keep people in education for a longer time. But this did not mean that the invisible ceiling that curbed social ascent had been removed. Even today, your social background will determine your possibilities in life; with the possible exception of professional footballers, actors and musicians (today's new aristocracy), your place in society will not be much different from the one your parents had. As early as the 1950s, when the educational reforms had just produced the first batches of alumni, it was evident that the reforms had not brought about the fundamental changes people had hoped for; enter the 'Angry Young Men' school of writers who expressed the bitterness this young generation felt; John Osborne's play *Look Back in Anger* best expressed their disillusionment, and writers such as Alan Sillitoe, John Wain or Harold Pinter were also associated with this group.

The well-to-do classes have always found ways to keep themselves to themselves: if you do not get into one of the better public schools, such as Eton, Harrow, Rugby, Winchester, Gordonstoun etc., and then proceed to Oxford or Cambridge, your career prospects are limited, particularly in politics and business.

Since the 1980s, the gap between the rich and the poor, the 'Haves' and the 'Chavs', has widened even more. I have already mentioned that during Maggie Thatcher's reign, the percentage of those living in poverty rose from 10 per cent to 25 per cent of the population. Today, a third of all children grow up in poverty. Poor people fall ill more often and die earlier than their better-off compatriots; teenage pregnancies are more numerous than in any other EU member country.

You might call these achievements a class act.

Brockworth, Gloucestershire

We look at sports in which the English can still beat the world

We stay on in the lovely Cotswolds and move across the county boundaries to Brockworth. The village does not have too many claims to fame – yes, it is an ancient place along the old Roman road connecting Gloucester and Cirencester, but no, this doesn't mean that you will find a village that is much different from the ones you find in other parts of England... except for one event that has brought fame and glory to the place: the annual 'Cooper's Hill Cheese-Rolling and Wake', which is held on the last Monday in May. And yes, it is about rolling large cheeses down a steep hill.

Most visitors to England will be familiar with the popular English sports; soccer is played all over the world, and you can find rugby and cricket in enough countries to make them truly international sports, too. There are also snooker and darts, and all the other sports you may have at home.

But most visitors will never have heard of the plethora of weird sports that the English indulge in. Cheese-rolling is just one of them.

The tradition of cheese-rolling goes back some two

hundred years and it was probably the invention of people who had imbibed a tankard or two of the strong stuff. To put it plainly, you must be hammered out of your mind to come up with the idea of taking a perfectly good, big cheese, throwing it down the hill and then chasing after it. He who crosses the finish line first is the winner and is rewarded with the cheese. The whole thing has been summarised by an Australian newspaper as 'twenty young men chase a cheese off a cliff and tumble 200 yards to the bottom, where they are scraped up by paramedics and packed off to hospital'.* This is a very fitting description; the procedure is not only insane, it is also dangerous. The cheeses are heavy and they go down the hill at a speed of more than 100 km/h. Any spectator knocked down by the thing may well end up in hospital, as do many of the 'athletes' – who tend to get some 'Dutch courage' in a nearby pub before the event.

If you are a bit yellow – as I am – or if your health insurance does not cover injuries sustained from pure stupidity, you may well choose the safest way to enjoy this sport: there is a cheese-rolling app for your smartphone.

For some reason, the Cotswolds seem to be the centre of weird sports in England; on the Friday following cheese-rolling day, you may enjoy the spectacle of the 'Cotswolds Olimpicks' near Chipping Camden, which were first introduced by a local lawyer in 1612. In the old days, the sports included were dull

---

* 'Return to edam'. *Sydney Morning Herald*, 13 November 2008.

affairs such as running, jumping or wrestling. After these fell out of favour in the mid-nineteenth century, the Olimpicks were revived and now include much more interesting disciplines, such as piano smashing, dwile flonking or shin kicking.

Dwile flonking is a quite intricate thing. It involves two teams, each taking it in turn to dance around the other while attempting to avoid being hit by a beer-soaked cloth, the 'dwile', which is thrown at them by the non-dancing team. Shin kicking is even more awe-inspiring; two men dressed in white coats kick at each other's shins (the rules outlaw steel-capped boots) until one of them falls down.

No, I did not make these things up.

Amesbury, Wiltshire

Where we look at old things.
Very old things indeed

We are headed for the West Country to look at the earliest traces of the people who much later became the English. As we know, every respectable nation tends to have its origins in the dark. With the English, there is not much darkness around. We are able to trace back the immigration to the islands for a very long time; we know who came when and from where and put paid to his predecessors. When it comes to ancestry, one might argue that the couple of thousand people living in what became England when the waves washed over the last remaining dry 'bridge' connecting it to the continent some 8,500 years ago, are the only true forefathers. But even pre-historic England had extensive contact with the rest of Europe and today's population is the result of constant extension of the gene pool by immigrants, from the Bronze Age to the Celts, from Romans to Anglo-Saxons and Vikings, the Normans and the later immigrants from Europe and the former colonies. Whether thousands of years of immigration have contributed to the lurking xenophobia amongst today's English is another matter altogether.

Genetic analyses have shown that today's English are most closely related to people living on the Iberian Peninsula. Which is not as astonishing as it sounds: 90 per cent of the European population can be traced back to seven genetic 'mothers' who themselves hailed from three distinct African clans. As for the Iberian roots, there are a number of possible explanations; maybe we are all related anyway, or it could be the result of immigration by hunter-gatherers in ancient times. Perhaps it was that the survivors of the Spanish Armada in 1588 expressed their joy at having been saved from cruel death in a rather enthusiastic way? I would doubt, however, that genetics are to blame for the English tendency to retire to the Algarve and Costa del Sol in such great numbers.

Back to the ancestors: The oldest remnants of humanoid creatures found in England date back some 200,000 years. In those days, the Thames was a mighty tributary to the Rhine; Neanderthal people roamed the land. Around 35,000 years ago, Homo Sapiens joined the roaming and whoever made it to this north-western outpost of Europe normally did so in pursuit of game and edible plants. If their pursuit took them too far, they ended up in Ireland and had to sing funny songs and learn Gaelic – life had its hardships even then.

The Ice Age came and went, forming the wonderful English landscape, and around 9,000 years ago Cheddar Man met his end and was buried in Cheddar Gorge near Bristol. His is the oldest complete skeleton that has been found in the British Isles. In those days, the maxim was 'waste not, want not', meaning that Cheddar Man's remains were used for Sunday roast. Pre-historic Englishmen were cannibals. Some years ago, genetic tests found three direct descendants of Cheddar Man: two schoolchildren and Adrian Targett, a teacher who lived less than a mile from the caves. We understand they do not share the culinary tastes of their forebears.

But we have already strayed too far, our trip takes us towards the lovely county of Wiltshire. There, less than half an hour's drive north of the cathedral city of Salisbury and just outside Amesbury, we find one of the most astonishing and mysterious monuments of a long-forgotten age: Stonehenge.

If you are a Druid or a member of some such New Age cult, you might have an idea about what Stonehenge actually was. For the rest of us, it is a mystery. Was it a temple of a sun cult? A prehistoric landing zone for spacecraft? A burial place? The name itself does not help us: *henge* is the Old English word for 'gallows' which in those times were constructed of two vertical posts, with a third one positioned horizontally on top from which to tie the rope. Stonehenge – the place of gallows made of stone?

One legend has it that the huge stones came from Africa and that the edifice was originally based in Ireland. The scheming wizard Merlin stole the whole thing, aided by one of those helpful giants who always come in handy when it comes to heavy lifting, and placed it in its present location. This legend may have its attractions, but it certainly does not have much truth to it. It goes to show, however, that the English had a liking for good crime fiction even before they knew they were English.

The truth is that to this day, we do not know what Stonehenge was built for, or who built it. But, with its famous stone circle and a large number of burial sites, it is the biggest and best preserved relic of the stone and bronze ages. These graves also indicate that the bulk of the construction was begun around 5,000 years ago, and there is evidence that some part of Stonehenge dates back as much as 7,000 years.

Stonehenge was in use for about 1,500 years and the site seems to have been constantly developed and enlarged during this time. The first and oldest part is formed by a circular ditch with a perimeter of approximately 110 metres. Animal bones and the remains of weapons and tools were found in some of the graves. Outside this circle, there are more than fifty holes in the ground, named 'Aubrey holes' after the man who discovered them. These seem to have held tree trunks or stones in the first couple of hundred years; they were later converted into graves.

The famous huge stones were erected around 2,600 BC, around the time the oldest Gizeh pyramids were built in Egypt. Archaeologists estimate that up to 80 of these giant monoliths were used; most of them have not remained on the site. Many of these rocks are of a type that does not naturally exist in Wiltshire; they must have come from the Welsh mountains. How were these giant rocks, which weigh in at more than four tonnes, transported here? Over in Africa, the

Egyptians had found methods of shifting huge pieces of stone over hundreds of miles, using ramps, boats, slave labour and the annual floods of the Nile. But there is no evidence that such techniques existed in England at the time and the general consensus is that the rocks that form Stonehenge were part of the rubble that was transported by ice age glaciers and left in the area when the ice receded.

Building work in and around Stonehenge continued for about 700 years, and even the waves of immigrants in the Bronze Age did not stop the continuous use of the structure. The entry to Stonehenge was relocated a number of times throughout this period until it came to its present position which is exactly aligned for the summer and winter solstices.

Development and construction at Stonehenge ceased around 1600 BC, but the site was used as a burial place for almost another 1,000 years. Roman artefacts and coins were also found here, but this is not considered proof of continued usage during these much later times.

There are still many mysteries surrounding Stonehenge, which was declared a World Heritage Site by UNESCO in 1986. This seemed highly necessary because, strangely enough, up until the twentieth century, the site did not receive much respect from the locals. Ownership of the place changed frequently; at some points it was in the monarch's possession, then it was handed over to private ownership and used as pasture. During World War II, an airstrip was built nearby and houses and a café were put up.

While Stonehenge was still in full usage, some semblance of civilisation came to England: the 'Beaker People' introduced dinnerware – which was not quite of Waterford quality yet. Although the beaker people would most certainly not have had collectors' editions with pictures of royal weddings or plants and birds, the English have kept their passion for crockery alive through the ages.

The Beaker People brought a lot of innovations; they did not eat their horses (well, not immediately) but rode them. They knew how to bake bread – the oldest English bread was discovered in Oxfordshire in 1999; it is more than 5,000 year old. Originally coming from the Rhineland, they also brought alcohol. Perhaps most importantly, they brought manufacturing skills; they knew how to spin wool and make textiles, how to process metal and shape it into tools and weapons and even how to make adornments of gold and amber. And thus England reached the Bronze Age.

Like almost everyone before and after them, the beaker people were immigrants – but they did not come over looking for food. The Beaker People were industrial immigrants and they were attracted by the copper and tin that was to be had on the island. We can presume that they were not greeted very enthusiastically by the existing inhabitants, but with their modern weaponry, they must have had some rather convincing arguments.

We tend to think of the people living in these pre-historic days as primitive, but Europe already had extensive trade links.

Excavations in Greece have found amber from Wessex in graves dating back to the Mycenaean period. Dishes and adornments used by the beaker people had ornamentation which closely resembled that found in Greece. So, our pre-historic friends really were active traders; another characteristic that has shaped the English through the ages, as Napoleon Bonaparte noted when he called the English 'a nation of shopkeepers'.

Life was good in the Bronze Age and everything seemed to be on the right track when methods for producing iron were developed. With modern tools, agriculture was revolutionised. Ploughing became much easier, more land was converted into fields and people started to settle for longer periods of time.

And then there were the Celts.

Ever since Asterix and Obelix stomped onto the stage, the image of the Celts has been closely linked to the characters created by Goscinny and Uderzo. We think of them as big guys, strong, aggressive and always ready to have a good fight. Which was true, actually: historic documents portray them as a bunch of hooligans who loved to fight in the nude and shout their lungs out in the process. Doesn't this remind us of English football fans?

Like the Beaker People before them, the Celts were industrial immigrants. Having run out of resources in their settlement areas in central Europe, they started to come to what they would later call Albion, in around 600 BC looking for ore (and probably for boar, as well).

The inhabitants of the Isles showed them the beauty spots, learned the language and assimilated the newcomers into the gene pool. The island in the North Sea became 'Britain' – an expression coined by the Greek writer Pytheas who wrote about the *Pretani*, the 'painted people' who inhabited the island. The Romans later latinised it: Britannia.

The Celts extended the trade links with Europe and excavations all over the continent have produced goods made in 'Olde England'. But Celtic dominance in Europe did not last long: Germanic peoples came to dominate the north of the continent; the Romans made the south their own. Many centuries later, we find the Celts pushed back to the fringes of the British Isles and into tiny areas on the continent.

Celtic languages have survived and can still be heard in the 'Six Celtic Nations': Ireland, Wales, Scotland, the Isle of Man, Cornwall and Britanny in France. But the last native speaker of Cornish died in 1777; the last native speaker of Manx in 1974; of Deeside Gaelic in 1984. In Ulster, part of which makes up Northern Ireland, there are more native speakers of Chinese than of Gaelic.

Wallsend, Tyne & Wear

*Omnes Britannia Romana and
the fury of a scorned woman*

We move on in our quest to find England, and it is to the north that we go. Ask any decent Londoner or inhabitant of the 'Home Counties' in the south about their ideas of the north, and they will probably shrug their shoulders. Even today, the north and south of England have not found common ground – northerners think of their southern compatriots as arrogant urban prats; the feeling is reciprocated in so far as southerners think of everybody living north of Oxford as being deeply rooted in the dark ages.

Whether this mutual resentment existed in Celtic times, we don't know. But when the Romans came and took over much of Britain, they faced a nasty shock: the Caledonians and Picts, who later became Scots, made a habit of coming down south for a bit of pillaging. So Emperor Hadrian ordered a wall to be erected to keep away these nasty people. Modelled upon the *limes* which runs through what is today central Germany, Hadrian's Wall was erected to seal off Roman Britain from the great unwashed northern hordes. It runs for approximately 120 kilometres (76 miles), from the Tyne in the east to the

48

Firth of Solway in the west, basically connecting today's cities of Newcastle and Carlisle.

But we have to slow down here: How did the Romans get to Britain? And why?

It was in the year 55 BC that Julius Caesar, who was conducting his Gallic Wars at the time, gave in to the urge to take a closer look at what lay beyond the Channel. Trade contacts between the Roman province of Gaul and Britain were long established – Caesar's legionnaires and his colonial administrators were particularly fond of the warm woollen clothes that came from 'Britannia', and the Celts on the other side of the Channel had developed a liking for the wine they were able to import in exchange.

As happens in business, one does not always have to like one's partner, and Caesar certainly did not feel the need for restraint when he described the Celts of Britain:

> The interior portion of Britain is inhabited by those of
> whom they say that it is handed down by tradition that they
> were born in the island itself: the maritime portion by those
> who had passed over from the country of the Belgae for the
> purpose of plunder and making war; almost all of whom
> are called by the names of those states from which being
> sprung they went thither, and having waged war, continued
> there and began to cultivate the lands. The number of
> the people is countless, and their buildings exceedingly
> numerous, for the most part very like those of the Gauls,

the number of cattle is great. They use either brass or iron rings, determined at a certain weight, as their money. Tin is produced in the midland regions; in the maritime, iron; but the quantity of it is small: they employ brass, which is imported. There, as in Gaul, is timber of every description, except beech and fir. They do not regard it lawful to eat the hare, and the cock, and the goose; they, however, breed them for amusement and pleasure. The climate is more temperate than in Gaul, the colds being less severe.

[...] The most civilised of all these nations are they who inhabit Kent, which is entirely a maritime district, nor do they differ much from the Gallic customs. Most of the inland inhabitants do not sow corn, but live on milk and flesh, and are clad with skins. All the Britons, indeed, dye themselves with woad, which occasions a bluish colour, and thereby have a more terrible appearance in fight. They wear their hair long, and have every part of their body shaved except their head and upper lip. Ten and even twelve have wives common to them, and particularly brothers among brothers, and parents among their children; but if there be any issue by these wives, they are reputed to be the children of those by whom respectively each was first espoused when a virgin.*

---

* '*De Bello Gallico*' & Other Commentaries of Julius Caesar', translated by W.A. MacDevitt. Everyman's Library, 1915. Quote from the Project Gutenberg online edition.

You could be excused for thinking that these people would have been ideal fodder for the average weekday afternoon talk show. Blue faces, polygamy, heavy moustaches – Caesar might have shrugged it off with a laconic *de gustibus non disputantur* and proceeded with other things. But there was this nagging issue of neighbourly love that the British Celts extended to their relatives on the continent, allowing the combatants from across the Channel to seek shelter whenever this was necessary. This was clearly annoying, especially for an up-and-coming politician such as Caesar, who had taken on his governorship in Gaul as a stepping stone towards higher office in Rome. So Caesar assembled an expeditionary force which landed in today's Kent, clearly expecting to walk over the enemy, teach them a lesson and be done with it. As it turned out, the local king Cunobelinus (upon whom William Shakespeare modelled his 'Cymbeline') had other ideas; the Celtic warriors sent the Romans clambering aboard their ships.

Caesar, being the PR professional that he was, knew well that a report of his adventure along the lines of 'I came, I saw, I got kicked in the teeth', would not have forwarded his career in any meaningful way. So he sat down and wrote one of the most astonishingly untrue accounts of what happened that has ever been written in world history. Rome was far away, mobile phones did not exist, so the Roman senate celebrated Caesar's 'victory' with a twenty day long feast.

This, of course, meant that Caesar had to deliver the goods eventually. And so, in the year 54 BC, a giant fleet of 800 ships sailed across the channel, with soldiers and weapons galore. The local king in charge, Casivelaunus, knew that this time there was not very much he could do, apart from sending home the bulk of his men and starting a guerrilla war. This seems to have gone rather well, but, as so often in politics, some other Celtic leaders thought that one shouldn't be too conservative and that a bit of modernisation *à la Romaine* could be quite interesting. So Casivelaunus was persuaded to hand himself over to Caesar, which he obviously did in style, as he was subsequently instated as Rome's chief ally.

And what did the mighty Caesar do next? Having come and looked around – and probably having been treated to dinner at some Celts' high tables – he upped sticks again, taking his soldiers with him. Whether it was because of the food or because he wanted to get back before the winter storms could wreak havoc upon his fleet, you decide. The Celts were left standing at the cliffs of Dover, watching the Roman fleet vanish into the sunset. Scratching their heads and shrugging their shoulders, they might have quoted Obelix: '*Ils sont fous, ces romains*' (Or, rather: '*Maent yn wallgof, y rhai Rhufeiniaid*', if his Welsh served him right). It is safe to assume that they did not shed too many tears and that they did not particularly miss their new Roman allies.

It took almost another hundred years before Emperor Claudius decided that Britain could be a nice addition to the Roman Empire. Even if the Celts tended to paint their faces blue, they had coal and ore and other things the Emperor wished to get his hands on. Claudius may not have been a soldier, but he took no chances: 40,000 legionnaires landed in Britain, which made the acting king, Caractacus, throw in the towel rather quickly. The Romans proceeded to Colchester, Celtic Britain's major town, and entered after a brief siege. They even had elephants in their parade, and I tend to agree with John O'Farrell that this was probably the most exciting thing ever to happen in Colchester.

Having established Roman rule, the new masters quickly set up four administrative zones, with the regional centres at York in the north-east, Lincoln in the middle, Cirencester in the south-west and the newly founded 'Londinium' in the south-east. This suited the Celts just fine because, by and large, this was congruent with existing boundaries. The local kings became Roman allies and apart from the fact that the old town of Colchester became off limits for Celts, life was alright. The new *cloacas* (sewers) seemed quite practical, togas became fashionable and the farmers did a roaring trade in *brassica*, the new cabbage that smart Celts just had to have.

And then came Boadicea.

The big statue of Boadicea on the northern head of Westminster Bridge shows a daunting warrior queen who might have been an ancient foremother of tough British women like Elizabeth I, the suffragettes or Lady Thatcher. Only cabbies find fault with the statue – just because the two horses drawing Boadicea's chariot are rearing in opposite directions, you will hear remarks about 'bloody women drivers, they're all the same'.

Whatever Boadicea's qualities as a chariot driver may have been, she certainly knew how to deal out a proper handbagging, as the Romans experienced when they crossed her in AD 61. Boadicea's husband, Prasutagus, had been one of the many local kings in today's East Anglia who had made a deal with the Romans: They left him in peace, and he promised to hand over half of his fiefdom when he met his maker. Such an arrangement was quite common, and it was mutually beneficial: it limited the number of colonial wars, the local rulers kept their dignity, and when the day of reckoning came, everybody involved was either happy or dead. So when Prasutagus died, the Romans were quite astonished to find that Boadicea sent them packing. Harsh words were exchanged and the Romans had the queen beaten up and her two daughters raped. At least, this is what the legend says.

If the legend is true, it was not only a move unfit for a Roman gentleman, but also a very stupid one. Boadicea's own Icenian people (and a number of friendly neighbours) hit back. For two years, the irate queen and her devoted warriors led a tough guerrilla campaign, plundering and burning down Roman settlements, including Londinium, which had only started its life twenty years prior to this. The effects of Boadicea's wrath are still visible in today's London; whenever deep foundations have to be dug for a new building, one comes across a layer of ashes and clay: Boadicea's layer.

In those days, Nero ruled in Rome and he almost pulled all his soldiers out of the rebellious province. Just before the marching orders were issued, the local governor mounted a last stand, assembling 10,000 soldiers who faced 230,000 Celts somewhere in the Midlands. Tacitus had Boadicea saying heroic words, which he did quite often, having the benefit of many years' hindsight. But it was no use: the Celts were vanquished. Boadicea and her daughters either died in battle, committed suicide or died of a mystery illness.

More than 80,000 Celts are said to have died in this last battle alone, along with tens of thousands of people living in the towns and settlements ravaged by the rebels. What a loss of life in a time when hardly a million people lived in Britain!

Boadicea was the last challenge to Roman rule in Britain from within. The other big challenge is the reason for our trip up north: the Scots.

Around AD 120, Emperor Hadrian visited Britain and found that colonial tranquillity and business were rudely disturbed from time to time by the Caledonians and Picts who, for some reason, could not be made to see the advantages of being ruled from Rome. To keep out these ancient Eurosceptics, Hadrian ordered his wall. For six years, legionnaires dug and shovelled – and probably ducked from the rain and shivered in the cold – and built the wall, which came with ditches, forts and watchtowers.

10,000 soldiers were stationed to protect the boundary, which probably made the Scots shake their heads in disbelief at the folly of the southerners, as they still do today. They shook their heads with good reason too, because the wall was never finished and there remained ample space to walk around it and venture south. The wall itself was of course the manifestation of a mighty empire having come to the end of its tether; the Romans could not beat the Scots, so they tried to keep them away. *Sic transit gloria imperii*, as one might have remarked.

Towards the fourth century, the wall had changed its function from barrier to customs inspection point: the canny Scots had found out that trading was more beneficial than pillaging for everyone involved. When the Romans left, the wall became a prime source for building materials, which is why you cannot see too much of it today. Reconstruction has been undertaken since the nineteenth century and the middle part especially is well worth a visit. Since 1987, Hadrian's Wall has been designated a UNESCO World Heritage Site and the path leading along it has become one of the most popular long-distance walks in the country.

If you venture up north, make sure to visit Wallsend near Newcastle. It is a rather dreary little town, but it does celebrate its Roman heritage by having street signs, posters and all sorts of things in both English and Latin. If you want to know what 'No Smoking' or 'Telephone' is in Latin, go there.

In *The Life of Brian*, John Cleese and his hapless band of freedom fighters argue about what the Romans have brought to Palestine, ending up with an endless list of achievements. Were this set in England, the list would have been much the same. The Romans brought proper streets and sewers, new technology and crafts, new forms of agriculture and new plants, such as apples, grape vines and roses. The population grew to almost two million, and there were goods to be had from all over the world and luxury to be lived in, for those who could afford it.

In the fourth century, English towns were completely romanised. 'Imperial' measurements such as pounds, feet and inches had been adopted, and the traffic kept to the left side of the famously straight streets, Roman style. Trade with Europe was booming; you could travel from Hadrian's Wall to Jerusalem using one currency, one language and one legal system. England exported ore and wool, and London became one of the biggest settlements in the empire. In Bath, the Romans had established a thriving spa resort using England's only hot thermal springs.

You can still see part of the old Roman wall in the City of London and whenever work starts on a new office building in central London, even more remnants of the Roman period are found. In 2001, a large treasure trove of 43 *aureii* was found. The coins showed the faces of ten different Roman emperors, from Nero to Marcus Aurelius, and they would have paid for five or six good quality slaves or 45,000 litres of wine.

Life was good in Roman England.

Jarrow, Tyne & Wear

We meet patient and not-so-patient invaders;
there are persons Venerable and Great;
we also learn of round tables and burning cakes

Having coaxed you into following me up north, we stay in the Newcastle area and head for Jarrow, just about two miles from Wallsend. This little town and its monastery, built in the late seventh century, became one of the foremost centres of learning in the early Middle Ages, owing to the work of the Venerable Bede; monk, scholar and chronicler of Anglo-Saxon history. He coined the term 'Anglefolk' to name his compatriots, and thus the English became English.

But once again, we mustn't be too hasty.

I left you with the Celtic Britons enjoying life in Roman splendour. But as always when the going is good for the English, they meet the Germans in the quarter finals. Think penalty shoot-out; think Paul Gascoigne's tears. Only this time around it was not about football.

The year AD 410 saw the Celts waving goodbye to the Roman legions. This moment is of some significance: while Caesar's invasion in the year 55 BC is the first definite date in British history, the year AD 410 brings us to the first true date in *English* history. It was the year in which Emperor Honorius declined to assist his British colonists against Anglo-Saxon raiders and called back all the legions stationed there to defend the empire against the Germanic hordes on the northern border. This left the Celts at the mercy of... more Germanic hordes.

What happened next is a matter of historical dispute: one school of thought says that the Angles, Saxons and Jutes, who had been waiting across the North Sea for quite some time, jumped into their boats and drove the Celts from their lands. There had indeed been numerous attempts by these Germanic tribes since AD 285 to get hold of the wealth and natural resources Roman Britain had to offer. Most of these attempts were thwarted by the Romans, who had built fortifications along the North Sea and channel coasts from Norfolk right to the Isle of Wight. Some historians argue that there had been Germanic settlements along the coast for quite some time and that the Anglo-Saxon take-over was evolutionary, with the new arrivals seizing the opportunity handed to them by the retreat of the Romans. Certainly the resulting Celtic upheavals made it easier for the Anglo-Saxons to enter Britain. Because the Celts wiped out the traces of their former colonial masters once they had regained their lands, Celtic tradition came back with a vengeance and Latin was not even retained as a *lingua franca*. Prominent among these Celtic traditions were petty wars between local kings who seized upon any opportunity to enlarge their fiefdoms. The cherished neighbours to the north had fun crossing the many gaps in Hadrian's Wall for the occasional pillaging trip, and in the west, similarly minded relatives came from Ireland and marauded the country.

The Celts in the street longed for peace, and some of their kings hired the most efficient mercenaries on offer: the Angles, Saxons and Jutes. Having been invited into Britain, they set about defending their paymasters' realms against intruders and gradually took over the country. Just like the Celts, the Anglo-Saxons did not show much respect for what remained of Roman civilisation – who needs aqueducts, sanitation systems and libraries? Stone houses were for wimps, timber and straw did the job just as well. And as long as there were roles of scripture to be had from the Roman libraries, there was a wonderful source of fuel to keep the fires burning.

When the Romans left, records stopped. England became England, and entered into the Dark Ages.

The Celts, who found themselves squeezed back into the hills and mountains in the north and west, were not happy. So they fought back, and they did it with literature. This should not surprise us today, given the Celtic reputation for song and poetry. So the story goes that King Arthur took a last look at Camelot and mounted his trusty steed to protect his land, his people and the Christian faith from the pagan hordes.

We all know the legends of Arthur and how he extracted his sword Excalibur from the stone; we know of the Knights of the Round Table, of Queen Guinevere and Lancelot, of Gawain and the Green Knight, of Merlin, Sir Galahad, the Quest for the Holy Grail and, of course, the tale of Arthur's last battle against Mordred upon which the king, mortally wounded, departs into the mists of Avalon.

Good stuff. But of course, as with journalism through the ages, one should not put it to the test of history. The written mentions of Arthur, in the work of the monk Nennius and Geoffrey of Monmouth, rely heavily on the myths and romances of the time. There are not many reasons to believe that a king called Arthur ever existed; even the concept of the knight was alien to the time and was only introduced to England after the Norman Conquest. Many of the tales which make up the legend are part of popular Celtic folklore and it was Geoffrey of Monmouth's *History of the British Kings*, written in 1138, which brought Arthur to literary life. The Arthurian stories were especially popular in France throughout the Middle Ages and enjoyed a tremendous revival from the nineteenth century onward, with novels by Mark Twain and others, countless movies, pop-rock (Rick Wakeman) and of course, Lerner and Loewe's musical, *Camelot*. And perhaps, had they been able to command the singing voice of Richard Harris, the Celts might have been in with a chance of fending off the Saxons.

Does it matter that King Arthur and his Knights almost certainly did not exist? I think not. The attraction of the legend lies in the romantic quest for a positive hero; the Knights of the Round Table and their heroic struggle portray virtues such as patriotism, charity and chivalry. Such virtues seem to have been scarce even in the Middle Ages, which explains the enormous success of the stories in those times.

Without even King Arthur to hold them back, the Anglo-Saxons spread out across the country. But it was not all struggle and strife: excavations have shown that Celtic Britons and their new masters lived and mingled peacefully in many places. You can trace the spread of the invaders from local place names: Essex, Sussex and Wessex are quite obviously Saxon areas. The settlements of the Angles are not as conspicuous; they settled in East Anglia (well, that one is quite obvious) and the kingdoms of Mercia, Bernicia and Deira. The Jutes made do with Kent and the Isle of Wight. Wales, Scotland and Cornwall became the retreat of those Celts who did not wish to mingle with the new rulers; in AD 780 King Offa remembered Hadrian's Wall and built 'Offa's Dyke' to keep out the Welsh.

I said previously that with the retreat of the Romans, records stopped. Our knowledge of what happened in the first 300 years of Anglo-Saxon England is based mainly on what we find in the chronicles written by the Venerable Bede. He is the founding father of historiography in England, and he is the reason why we have chosen to come to Jarrow to find out about this section of English history.

Bede was a true Geordie: born in the village of Wearmouth, he spent all his life in the area, joining the new abbey as a nine-year-old boy. At this time, living in a monastery was much safer and more comfortable than eking out one's existence in the service of a feudal landlord. Bede learnt a lot and wrote voraciously: religious texts, poems, text books, treatises on nature and science, including calculations of the influence the moon has on the tides.

But his outstanding work is his *Historia Ecclesiastica Gentis Anglorum*, the first historical account of the 'Anglefolk', the English people, reaching back to the times of Julius Caesar. His *Historia* is a treasure trove of information, and it made history in another sense: Bede was the first historian to use the year of Christ's birth as reference point. The good people of Jarrow honour Bede with a pleasantly sophisticated theme park: 'Bede's World' gives a fine impression of what life in the early Middle Ages must have been like, with reconstructed houses and a lovely herb garden.

The Anglo-Saxons set up seven major kingdoms, which all included smaller fiefdoms. All of them were constantly at each other's throat, and there is a confusing array of short-lived kings: sons killed their fathers, brothers killed each other and even the odd aunt proved competent at wielding a dagger or using the strategic poison flask. Northumbria, Mercia and Wessex eventually emerged victorious, having swallowed the competition from East Anglia, Essex, Kent and Sussex by AD 850.

The rivalry between the kingdoms did not much help to beat off the sea-faring neighbours from Scandinavia who had discovered that there were nice things to be had in disunited England: the Vikings came, they killed and they plundered. By AD 865, the Great Pagan Army of Norsemen had landed in East Anglia and ten years later, Northumbria and Mercia were history.

This left Wessex and its king to fight the cause of the Anglo-Saxons and it did not look as if this could last very long. The king had to take refuge in the swampy lowlands of Somerset. But, as it transpired, things did turn out well – because Alfred was Great.

Alfred, King of Wessex (AD 849–899), is the only king in English history to be given the epithet 'Great'. There are two main reasons: he fought back the Vikings and he took the first major steps towards uniting the country – not only with the sword, but also with the power of the legal codex, the *Book of Dooms*, which combined Christian, Celtic and Saxon traditions.

Alfred had never thought of becoming king; he was the fourth son of Ethelwulf (many Anglo-Saxon nobles had names starting with 'Ethel-'; it is Saxon for 'noble') and had been busy preparing for a career in the church. He only got to the throne after all of his older brothers had died in battle. Not being a natural warrior, he tried to pay the Vikings off with a handsome tribute, but this only kept them at bay for two years. When they came back, Alfred's troops were defeated and the king went into hiding.

And this is where one of the nicer stories in English history begins: sheltering anonymously with a family of farmers, Alfred was given the task of overseeing the baking of cakes. Well, kings don't really do cooking, and so the farmer's wife returned to find the cakes all burnt. This bumbling incompetence immediately proved his nobility; Alfred said sorry (as Englishmen do) and started building a guerrilla army.

Alfred's battles against the Vikings lasted until AD 896, with only short periods of peace in between. In this time he established a semi-professional army, set up a navy and reformed the judiciary. In the 880s, the country was officially partitioned: Alfred held onto to the south-west; the northern and eastern parts, including London, were ruled by the Vikings – today, the region is still occasionally referred to as 'the Danelaw'.

Alfred was the first to call himself King of England, although he only controlled a third of the country. He died in AD 899; his remains were first buried in Winchester and later brought to the abbey in Hyde. When Henry VIII confiscated the Catholic Church's assets, Alfred's tomb was looted. His coffin and the grave goods were melted down and the king's bones were interred in an anonymous grave.

The world is an unfair place, as the comedian Mark Steel remarked: Alfred unified the English, created a working judiciary and turned a country ravaged by war into a functioning entity. And what do the people talk about? Of course, the Burning of the Cakes.

Alfred fought the Vikings throughout his lifetime, and his successors did not enjoy better relations with the unruly mariners. But the king had learnt an important lesson: England had to be united to be able to fend off threats from abroad. This is why he put together his *Book of Dooms*, and this is why he styled himself 'King of England'. His heirs understood this, and it was his son Æthelstan who managed to combine all three Anglo-Saxon kingdoms for the first time in AD 927, if only for a few years.

If anybody thought that with Alfred's achievements and compromises, the Viking threat would be over, he would have found himself severely mistaken. Right up until the end of Anglo-Saxon rule in England, the Norsemen played a major role in the fate of the realm. King Ethelred the Unready (meaning, the ill-advised) managed to lose his kingdom, only to regain it when the Viking King Sweyn died. Ethelred's son, Edmund Ironside, died early and another Viking took over, this time King Canute.

Canute, whose reign from 1016 to 1035 brought a semblance of stability, became famous for a stunt that has left many people puzzled over the years: one day he ordered his nobles to accompany him to the beach, just as the tide came in. He let his throne be placed right where the waves would wash over the shoreline and, being the sovereign master of his realm, commanded the water neither to rise on to his land, nor to wet his clothes. The sea, probably out of a republican whim, chose not to obey the command, and the king had to be rescued from further damage.

Why did he do it? Canute was a fierce warrior who thrived in battle, adding Denmark and Norway to his possessions, thus establishing one of the largest European kingdoms in post-Roman times. This is why his folly was sometimes interpreted as an act of gross arrogance. But there is also a completely different explanation: Canute knew that he had to reconcile

Anglo-Saxon and Viking interests and he did so by appointing local governors, the 'jarls' – this is where today's 'earl' has its origin – and county administrators, the 'shire-reeves' (today's 'sheriffs'). So Canute's declaration, standing dripping wet on the beach, attains an interesting meaning: according to the chronicler Henry of Huntingdon, whose *History of the English* was completed in 1130, Canute reminded his followers that 'the power of kings is empty and worthless'; God was the one true ruler and the only one who could command the sea. Here was a king who deliberately exposed himself to ridicule – making a point to emphasise the importance of the bond between the Crown, the nobility of the land and their faith.

Upon Canute's death, England entered into another prolonged era of strife as the powerbrokers of the realm jostled for position. Edward the Confessor, Canute's successor, eventually died without leaving an heir. Harold Godwinson, the Duke of East Anglia, who had also brought Wessex under his control, was the obvious contender for the throne, not least because he was also the late king's brother-in-law.

It was the year 1066. Harold's joy was not to last long.

First, the old friends from Norway discovered that they might be in with a chance: King Harald (with an 'a') was also related to Canute and Harold's brother, Tostig, joined the Norseman. 'Family!', Harold sighed and directed his troops towards York, which had been sacked by the advancing army. The battle was brief, Harold was victorious – and just had time for a clean-up and probably a drink when the next disastrous bit of news was delivered: the Normans had landed on the south coast.

William 'the Bastard', Duke of Normandy, had found that he too had a good claim to the English throne and had brought his troops across the channel. Harold made his troops march the 400 kilometres south to Hastings in the record time of thirteen days and launched into battle. The result changed world history: the English troops were tired, but gave a good fight. Harold was killed in action – whether by an arrow to his eye, as the Bayeux Tapestry suggests, or by other means does not really matter. William 'the Bastard' became William the Conqueror. And the English had to learn some French.

Beaker People and Celts, Romans, Angles, Saxons, Jutes, Vikings and Normans – the first couple of thousand years of England's history saw many conquerors making the island their home. This had now come to an end; since 1066, many others have tried to conquer England – Vikings, the Spanish and even Herr Hitler – and they have all failed.

York, Yorkshire

We hear about angels and Angles,
find the Lord and look at a lot of glass

W̲e have heard a lot about pre-Norman English history, but we have so far missed out on one of its most important elements: the advent of Christianity in England. To learn more about this, we stay in the north of England and travel to York, the pleasant city by the River Ouse, which is home to the second most important 'province' in the Church of England.

Founded by the Romans in AD 71, York soon became the administrative capital of the north, although it did not receive its present name until the seventh century, when the Vikings made 'Jorvik' their stronghold. Christianity had been the official religion throughout the Roman Empire, and therefore in the British colony as well, since AD 313 following the Edict of Milan, and York became a bishopric soon after. But Christianity may have been around for a while by then. According to reports picked up by the Venerable Bede, missionaries came to Britain as early as AD 180 on the invitation of a Celtic king, Lucius. According to these reports, Christianity spread quickly and only came to a temporary halt when Emperor Diocletian imposed a major clamp-down.

This sounds good; probably too good to be true. The whole story may come down to a medieval scribe mixing up 'Britain' and 'Britium' – which is in today's Turkey.

Whether the story of early Christianity is true or not, for almost 500 years, Christianity remained very much a niche religion. The spreading of the gospel would not have been helped much by the retreat of the Romans in AD 410; neither the Anglo-Saxons nor the Vikings were very eager to convert. Some parts of the Celtic population stayed true to the faith, establishing a distinct brand of Christianity, which differed from the Roman version of Catholicism that came to England much later.

Legend has it that the Roman Catholic push into England is due to a chance encounter at a slave market in Rome. One day, Bishop Gregory, who later became Pope, came across a group of exceptionally handsome young men. When he asked where they came from, he was told that they were Angles. 'Non Angli sed *angeli*' was his reply – 'not Angles but angels', which only goes to show that punning is indeed an old vice. Gregory must have been very impressed by his own joke because, when he finally got his promotion, he sent out missionaries to qualify these 'angels' for heaven.

The most efficient of these missionaries was Augustine, who, at Gregory's behest, blended many of the old myths and symbols of his flock with the new beliefs, rededicating holy wells and places of pagan worship to Christian saints. The strategy worked well: King Ethelbert of Kent, who had married the Christian princess Bertha of France, converted in AD 601; by AD 655, the last remaining pagan king, Penda of Mercia, had died. By then, the differences between the Celtic and Roman versions of Catholicism had become clear and the Synod of Whitby (AD 664), just a couple of miles away from York, had to be called to reconcile these differences. Once again, the Celts lost out to their former colonial masters; the Roman version was accepted as the guideline on questions such as when to celebrate Easter and how to shave the monastic tonsure.

By this time, the first church on the site of today's York Minster had been built – a humble edifice of wood, which was quickly replaced by a stone building more befitting the seat of a bishop. Today's York Minster is the result of building work which started in 1220 – the incumbent archbishop obviously felt the urge to put one over his colleague in Canterbury. He did not see his ambitions fulfilled: building works took more than 250 years and the first full service was not held until 1472. York Minster is the second largest church north of the Alps (only Cologne's Dome is bigger); it is 160 metres long, the towers are 60 metres high and some parts of it go back to the second rebuilding of the edifice, which started in AD 741. The special highlight of the building is the beautiful Great East Window (finished in 1408), the largest expanse of medieval stained glass in the world.

The – voluntary – first demolition of the old church set the tone for what happened over the coming centuries; time and again the cathedral was destroyed, owing to the fact that the city itself changed hands between Anglo-Saxons and Vikings on several occasions. When the Normans took over, they too left their mark on York by doing some major damage to the church. The bad-luck-blighted story of York Minster continues to the modern day: the most recent large fire happened in 1984.

The Tower of London

*Where ghosts, birds and public records
are our concerns*

The Norman Conquest brought the last decisive ingredient to the English language as we speak it today: French, or rather, the Norman version of French. Just as the Vikings had been the scourge of many English kings, so had they sunk their teeth into northern France. Whereas in England, Vikings and Anglo-Saxons never found a lasting way of coexisting, the French kings understood that it was in their best interests to appease the unruly men from up north by ceding part of the country to them – similar to the Danelaw era in England, which had seen the north and east of the country under the rule of the Danish Vikings, but different inasmuch as the Normans were integrated into the French tributary system. William the Bastard's claim to the English throne came through the common Viking family history that he shared with the deposed King Harold; both were related to King Canute.

One would have thought that the Normans would have stuck to their Scandinavian dialect but over the years, they took on the ancient French of the land. Upon coming to

England, they quickly secured their position through strategic marriages and relied on a small number of talented Anglo-Saxons, who took on the administration of their new masters' possessions. This, of course, meant that one had to communicate and thus, over the years, both languages merged into what became modern English.

Once he had taken hold of his new realm, William the Conqueror needed to bring it under his firm control. This could not be done with a relatively small number of soldiers in London, so William brought Norman barons with him and gave them the run of the shires. The favour was not granted to just any Norman nobleman; William relied on a relatively small number of trusted allies, relatives and friends – fewer than 30,000 Normans took over the management of two million Anglo-Saxons and Danes. Just eleven mighty provincial nobles reigned over more than half of England.

Every one of William's nobles had to build a fortification in a strategic place, where soldiers could be stationed and from which the region could be administrated; tax collecting had become the natural pastime for whoever was in power, be it Celts, Romans, Anglo-Saxons or Normans. (I have already told you about how the ancient Tally Sticks were instrumental in the rebuilding of the Palace of Westminster; they came into use around this time.) Over the next 25 years, the new rulers built around 100 of these fortifications, some of which developed from makeshift wooden forts into mighty castles. Windsor Castle is one of these early Norman fortifications, as is Warwick Castle and the Tower of London, possibly England's most famous medieval building.

William I started work on the Tower just months after coming to England. It was the visible proof that the Powers That Be had, indeed, changed. For the first time, London received something like a skyline: the castle overlooked old Saxon London and stood out impressively to the river traffic on the Thames.

From the beginning, William I insisted upon the strongest possible defences and his architects made clever use of what they found; the earliest part of the Tower uses the old Roman town walls and the river as boundaries and protection. The Tower oozed power and aggression, and Londoners hated it, correctly perceiving it as a symbol of oppression.

The tower served quite a number of purposes during its history, most notably as royal residence, as well as a jail for high-profile prisoners. It was also, at various times, an armoury, a treasury, home of the Royal Mint and the Public Records Office. Many nobles and not-so-nobles were executed here, but only a few met their maker within the walls of the Tower. The majority of the executions took place outside the gates, on Tower Hill. As a royal residence, it was used for almost 500 years, until Henry VII found it rather too uncomfortable for his needs.

Today's Tower, with its combined usage as storage for the crown jewels and as a tourist trap, is among the capital's biggest attractions. Quaint traditions like the daily Ceremony of the

Keys add to the Tower's allure, as do the Beefeaters (officially Yeoman Warders) and the ravens; at least six of them are kept at the Tower at all times because, so the legend says, once the ravens leave the tower, the kingdom will fall. There are also quite a number of ghosts haunting the Tower, or so one is told: Anne Boleyn is said to be there, Henry VI and, of course, the 'little princes' who were most probably murdered in the Tower at the behest of their wicked uncle, Richard III.

William's policy of installing an exclusively Norman aristocracy created a huge upheaval of the traditional structures. Those Anglo-Saxon nobles who did not agree to play second fiddle to the new rulers were deprived of their possessions, driven off the land or killed. The entire aristocratic system was changed to reflect Norman customs, which had of course been moulded on the French way of doing things. Thus many of the English forests became off-limits to the population – the Norman aristocrats loved hunting and did not want to share the spoils with local peasants. Despite this upheaval, William I adopted the laws codified by Alfred the Great and explicitly ruled that these existing laws should remain in force – for the English. To 'all men I have brought with me, or who have come after me', he extended special royal protection; one set of rules for the rulers, another one for the ruled; nice!

Whereas the lower ranks of the Norman aristocracy were busy merging their language with that which was spoken by their subjects, the higher echelons of Norman nobility found it rather undignified to speak any language but French – a sentiment you will find ingrained in today's France as well. The insistence on French as the language of authority and dominance has left traces in today's English: 'police', 'judge', 'execution', and 'court' are all French in origin. But they had a proper excuse for their ignorance of the Anglo-Saxons' English: officially being vassals of the French king, the dukes of Normandy and barons of smaller areas had huge holdings not only in England, but also in the 'old country' across the channel as well, and they held onto them for almost 500 years. Through this system, the new English king's authority reached from Ireland through Wales and England and as far south as the Spanish border.

Another major addition the Normans brought to England's social structures was the 'knight'. These mounted warriors had been a sought-after Norman export for a number of years. The idea of a chivalrous knight, such as in the Ivanhoe legend, would have seemed ridiculous to these men; they were renowned for their complete lack of scruples and served as mercenaries to whoever paid good money. Harold's predecessor, Edward the Confessor, had hired Norman knights to fight the Welsh, with limited success. The knights were also very actively engaged in the crusades, which produced a gaggle of short-lived Norman kingdoms in the Middle East and along the Mediterranean coast.

Conquering England went down in world history as a major feat, but in addition to his military influence, William I also revolutionised national administration with his *Domesday*

Book, which was put together in 1087. This was the first statistical record of its kind that had been undertaken anywhere in Europe in post-Roman times. The upside was evident: ever since the conquest there had been disputes between the Crown and its tributaries over who owned what. While the Anglo-Saxon kings had been mainly content with ruling the country, the Norman idea was that the Crown actually owned it. Everybody had to pay his duty to the Crown and for the first time, the records provided the government with a basis for calculating the tax and duties it could expect to receive. On nine hundred pages, the *Domesday Book* recorded each person's individual holdings for eternity – hence its name. His Majesty's subjects may have been loyal, but they certainly were not happy about the snooping.

The *Domesday Book* had some strange omissions – the cities of London and Winchester were not accounted for, as well as some parts of the North East. But nevertheless, it is a fantastic document that gives an insight into the time: there were 13,418 settlements and approximately two million people; 65 per cent of England was used as farmland and pasture, 15 per cent was forested (today only 7 per cent of England is forested).

His *Domesday Book* completed, William I left his earthly realm for pastures new. His successors mainly consolidated their positions of power, and they weren't fussy when it came to the means. William the Conqueror's heir, William II, lost his life in a hunting accident in the New Forest in 1100.

By coincidence, his younger brother Henry happened to be nearby with the two brothers-in-law of the man who actually released the fatal arrow that killed the king; the culprit immediately fled to France and was never prosecuted over the incident. Henry I founded England's first zoo and then took on his oldest brother, Robert '*Courtheuse*' ('Shortstockings'), who had inherited the Duchy of Normandy, and wrested from him control over the native province of England's ruling elite. Today, members of the English elite (and well-to-do pensioners) emulate Henry's move by buying up houses in Normandy. Oh, tradition!

When his only legitimate son died in a shipwreck, Henry was left without an obvious heir. He declared that his daughter Matilda would succeed him. Although the barons agreed to respect his wishes, it was not long after his death that his nephew, Stephen of Blois, seized the throne from Matilda. After many years of bitter conflict, Matilda and Stephen signed the Treaty of Winchester, agreeing that Matilda's son, Henry, would be the next king. Stephen honoured the agreement and even had the decency to die within a year, at which point Henry II was crowned.

Henry II made it very clear that he insisted on keeping his footing in France by marrying the Duke of Aquitaine's daughter, which gave him control over half of France and propelled him onto the stage of true European power politics. Within England, he reformed the legal system, introducing the Viking custom of juries into the courts and making his judges travel throughout the land to hold 'assizes', the sessions of the court. Helped by his loyal friend and chancellor, Thomas Becket, he even tackled the tradition that all church officials were exempt from the common law; until that point, if a monk stole or killed or raped, he could only be tried by the church. The church, of course, opposed the idea of being subject to the law of the land, and so it must have seemed a sign from heaven when the obstinate Archbishop of Canterbury died in 1161, clearing the path for the appointment of Thomas Becket.

But if the King had thought that this would ease his problems with the church, he was very much mistaken: Becket, the ever loyal workaholic and famously worldly friend immediately resigned from his post as chancellor and started to defend the ancient rights of the church with intense vigour against the King's plans. Henry II was astonished and dismayed. Feathers were ruffled, hard words were exchanged; Becket went into exile for six years, returning in 1170 to continue getting on the King's nerves. When Becket condemned to hell all those who had taken part in a crowning ceremony for Henry's son, the King is said to have uttered the words that should have been left unspoken: 'Will no man rid me of this turbulent priest?' – the true words are reported to have been somewhat different, but they achieved the desired effect. Four Norman knights in shining armour set out for Canterbury and duly reunited the archbishop with his ultimate boss. The Catholic Church, always quick to make a buck, swiftly made Becket a saint and turned Canterbury into a thriving pilgrimage destination.

Sherwood Forest, Nottinghamshire

*We meet men in tights and
a very unfortunate lion*

The most telegenic of the early Norman kings is undoubtedly the suitably-monikered Richard the Lionheart. The first of the royal Richards, he ascended into common lore and later into Hollywood, most often cast as a saintly *deus ex machina*-figure, hero of the English, whose appearance towards the end of the movie saves the hero's skin. In reality, Richard I was true to the tradition of the Norman kings: he did not speak a word of English and divided his time between France and the crusades. During the ten years of his reign, he spent about six months in England.

Richard's most important contribution to the well-being of England came when he let himself be captured on his return journey from the crusade. One of many legends reports that Richard received his nickname during this imprisonment at Castle Durnstein in today's Austria, by fending off a hungry lion that had been brought into his cell and tearing the animal's heart out. This act would certainly have made an impression on his captors, but the King's ransom was not altered, and it was indeed a king's ransom: 100,000 silver marks, or 23 tonnes of silver. As we know from reading the *National Enquirer* and other media of note, royal families, and kings and queens in particular, do not travel with cash on them. So, the trusty English subjects of His French-speaking Majesty had to cough up the money, which represented more than a year's worth of tax and duty income. The effects of this incident were disastrous: England was in dire financial straits. Poverty, which had never been far from people's doors, struck with a vengeance.

As has been the case in English history over the centuries, legend came to the fore. Richard the Lionheart's era spawned the stories of Robin Hood, the noble robber who took from the rich to give to the poor. What a noble character! And how enduring; much of the more aggressive rhetoric we hear today when it comes to bankers' bonuses seems to owe its metaphors to the deeds of Robin and his Merrie Men, who were said to dwell in Sherwood Forest.

Sherwood Forest is an impressive patch even today, but it must have been overwhelming in the days of Richard I, when traditional lore told of all sorts of wondrous things happening there. The area has been forested since the end of the Ice Age, and it was used as a royal hunting ground, the 'shire wood' of Nottinghamshire, which extended far into the neighbouring shires.

But, of course, all the stories about the noble robbers are balderdash; Robin Hood almost certainly never existed, which does not prevent the good people of Nottingham from naming their airfield 'Robin Hood Airport'.

There are, in fact, numerous reports of gangs roaming the English forests in the twelfth and thirteenth centuries and there are also court records from York, which mention a case brought against an outlaw named 'Rob Hod' in 1225. But the name, in a number of variations, soon spread throughout the country and seems to have been used as a generic term for the outlaws roaming the forests. Many of these gangs were driven to crime by the poverty and deprivation that had befallen the rural population, following the King's ransom payment. You may remember that many forests had been turned into hunting grounds for Norman nobility; they were off limits to ordinary people. If a person was found to have hunted in the forbidden forests, or even to have been carrying a bow and arrows, penalties such as castration or death were meted out. In a time of severe economic distress, closing the forests put the lives of the people living in these areas at risk. The Norman nobility could not care less.

The first stories and ballads about the noble robber appeared around 1300. Most of them sang his praise as a rebel against the rule of John 'Lackland', Richard's brother. He was the Regent of England while the King was gallivanting about in the Middle East on his crusades, and he eventually ascended the throne in 1199. As time went by, Robin changed from deprived peasant to deprived member of the aristocracy; the balladeers obviously mixed snippets of other folktales into the plot. Actually, England's Robin Hood is not alone; other nations have similar figures and legends – there is Wassilij,

'God's Fool' in Russia; the Japanese have Ishikawa Goemon; in the Ukraine, Ustym Karmaliuk does the noble deeds and in Germany, Schinderhannes kept fooling the authorities.

Robin's entourage grew in keeping with his ever-improving ancestry. Little John, Will Scarlet and Much the Miller's Son started off the gang; Maid Marian and Friar Tuck joined the happy band in the sixteenth century. By that time, Robin Hood, who had always been portrayed as a positive, if criminal, character, had attained the saintly habit of robbing the rich to give to the poor. He had become part of show business: balladeers made a humble living from the songs and legends about him and, as with journalism throughout the ages, it was a case of if the story works, don't worry about the facts too much. And if you can get the likes of Errol Flynn and Kevin Costner to act as men in tights, you're in with a winner!

Runnymede, Surrey

We learn of kings lacking in brains and land;
we meet the Prince of Wales and
wave two fingers at the French

Just a few miles west of central London, we come to visit a spot that has a special place in the history of politics: Runnymede, a flood plain along the River Thames. It was here where John I signed the 'Magna Carta', the first document that granted certain inalienable rights to a king's subjects.

When Richard the Lionheart died, odious John acceded to the throne and proved, as he had done during his time as Regent, that he was not up to the job. It took him only a short time to come to loggerheads with his relatives in France, the Pope and his vassals in England. Being a king, you are allowed to get into a scuffle with whoever you like – but you had better be successful. John wasn't.

In 1215, the Anglo-Norman nobility had reached the end of their tether. They set up an army and marched on London, where the inhabitants jubilantly opened the gates and welcomed them. They had a good talk with King John; he was either to sign a contract that gave far-reaching rights to the aristocracy or – well, there may have been some meaningful rattling of swords.

John understood and signed one of the greatest legal documents in world history, the Magna Carta. It stipulated that the king was subject to the rule of law and could only rule with the consent of his people. These people would be represented by 25 barons – 'people' back then did not mean John the farmer or Bill the factory worker.

But, at least in theory, everybody now had far more rights: the right to habeas corpus was entrenched, nobody could be imprisoned without reason, and no man could be sentenced in a court of law on the evidence of a woman (the English judiciary sometimes seems to be particularly sentimental about this provision). These and other rules laid down in the Magna Carta were adhered to until the nineteenth century, and they still form the basis of English law, as well as the US Constitution.

The consensual rule set out in the Magna Carta did not cause too many problems for most kings following John, but it came in very handy more than 400 years later, for the trial of Charles I who lost first the support of parliament, then the Civil War, and finally his head.

But we are running ahead of ourselves; we're still with John. He tried to show his barons his true mettle and reneged on the deal almost before the ink had dried. As they still had their weapons to hand, they started a civil war, which put paid to John's ambitions. The defeated king did the best he ever did for the realm by dying just a year later. His son, Henry III, took over, aged nine at the time. He reigned for 56 years, the longest period any English king managed in the Middle Ages.

Henry III consolidated the claim of the Plantagenets to the English throne; the descendants of the family stayed in power until 1485, producing fifteen kings. York Minster and Westminster Abbey were built, along with many other magnificent churches and castles. The Plantagenets also granted consent for the founding of the universities in Oxford and Cambridge, and they invaded Wales and claimed it for England.

When Edward I, Henry III's son, established English rule in Wales, it was suggested to him that he needed to placate the unruly Celtic neighbours. So he promised that the next king would be born in Wales and would not speak a word of English; he kept his promise by taking his pregnant wife across the border to deliver her first-born there. Since then, tradition prescribes that the heir to the English throne bears the title 'Prince of Wales'.

The invention of the Prince of Wales shows the cunning that was evident throughout Edward's reign. When the Scots started a liberation struggle, he produced the script for Mel Gibson's *Braveheart* by capturing William Wallace and having him executed. At the same time, he instigated fierce suppression of the Jews living in England, even forcing them to wear a yellow felt star in public – a nasty practice found all over medieval Europe that Herr Hitler brought back some 660 years later. (The English also invented concentration camps, much later, during the Boer War.) Edward needed money and the Jews, who had been lured to England by William I, controlled the money markets. They were the backbone of the English economy and they were easy prey, as they were direct subjects of the king. In 1275, Edward issued the 'Statute of Jewry', which made life and business extremely hard. There had already been pogroms against the Jewish communities in England, as well as in the rest of Europe, but in 1290, Edward I formally banned them from his kingdom, giving them only limited time to make their way across the Channel. Many of the captains who agreed to transport Jews to the continent abandoned their passengers on the Dogger Bank, the largest sand bank in the North Sea; thousands drowned.

Lest we forget: the Plantagenet kings of England were still owners of huge parts of France, and when that country's king died in 1337, they thought it might be a good and reasonable idea to take over that throne too.

The idea may have been reasonable, but it certainly was not good. All over France, battles were fought until 1458; the Hundred Years War had begun. Do not be misled by the name; for most of the time, there were no actual battles. It only means that it took a very long time to resolve the dispute. It was a nasty business, but 'the troubles' (as today's spin doctors would call them) in France led to the creation of legends on both sides: Joan of Arc for the French, Agincourt for the English.

'Agincourt' still features heavily in the English self-image as an hour of particular triumph. It is seen as having set the stage for many more events where the English would prove victorious when faced with powerful adversaries. Would this event have been transformed into legend without the words of the Bard, who has King Henry V rally his men with an adrenaline-pumping speech?

This day is called the feast of Crispian:
He that outlives this day, and comes safe home,
Will stand a-tip-toe when the day is named,
And rouse him at the name of Crispian.
He that shall live this day, and see old age,
Will yearly on the vigil feast his neighbours,
And say 'To-morrow is Saint Crispian:'
Then will he strip his sleeve and show his scars.
And say 'These wounds I had on Crispin's day.'
Old men forget: yet all shall be forgot,
But he'll remember with advantages
What feats he did that day: then shall our names.
Familiar in his mouth as household words
Harry the king, Bedford and Exeter,
Warwick and Talbot, Salisbury and Gloucester,
Be in their flowing cups freshly remember'd.
This story shall the good man teach his son;
And Crispin Crispian shall ne'er go by,
From this day to the ending of the world,
But we in it shall be remember'd;
We few, we happy few, we band of brothers;
For he to-day that sheds his blood with me
Shall be my brother; be he ne'er so vile,
This day shall gentle his condition:

And gentlemen in England now a-bed
Shall think themselves accursed they were not here,
And hold their manhoods cheap whiles any speaks
That fought with us upon Saint Crispin's day.

William Shakespeare, *Henry V*, Act 4, Scene 3

Great words! And thanks to the power of Laurence Olivier's delivery in the movie that was produced in 1944, they even served as a rallying cry in the Second World War.

At Agincourt, about 6,000 English soldiers fought off the French enemy, whose ranks counted some 25,000 troops. Crucial to the victory were the 4,000 archers on the English side, who used their longbows – the deadliest weapon of the time – with lethal precision on the foe who came stumbling across a muddy plane. It was a massacre: at the end of the day, more than 7,000 French had been killed, many of them noblemen. Just 200 English soldiers had lost their lives. The English archers waved their index and middle fingers at the enemy – the French had the habit of cutting off the fingers of captured archers. Thus, on a rainy day in 1415, the traditional salute of the English football hooligan was created.

At the time of the Battle of Agincourt, the Plantagenets had already been sidetracked by domestic feuds over succession. The romantically named 'Wars of the Roses' were fought between the houses of Lancaster and York, and over the next 80 years both houses provided the realm with three kings each.

You will know about the shenanigans that went on if you are familiar with Shakespeare's History Plays, but you should also bear in mind that history tends to be written by the victors – Shakespeare's hatchet job on Richard III, in particular, may have been a piece of Tudor-era spin doctoring.

Just bear with me for a little detour here: Richard III's opening speech in the play starts with the words, 'Now is the Winter of our Discontent / Made glorious summer by this sun of York.' Some years ago I came across a huge poster advertising outdoor gear with the slogan: 'Now is the discount of our winter tents' – show me a finer example of classic drama put to hilarious use!

As a result of the feuds at home and abroad, the Plantagenets lost out completely: by 1485, France had been lost for good, as was the English throne, which was now occupied by Henry (VII) Tudor – grandson of Henry V's widow, Catherine of France and of her Welsh clerk of the chamber, Owain ap Maredudd ap Tewdwr (or: Owen, son of Meredith, son of Tudor). Having close ties to the House of Lancaster himself, Henry VII married Elizabeth of York, proving that a little bit of clever marriage diplomacy can do a world of good.

Southwark, London

We give you a new Church, a Virgin Queen and the Bard of bards; and we wave goodbye to the Middle Ages

Looking across the Thames from the Tower of London, we have glimpsed a number of strange buildings. We cross the river using Tower Bridge (if you have the time, do go inside and marvel at the technology) and, walking west along the south bank of the river, we eventually reach the Globe Theatre. The construction itself is a little gem in an area that features a gaggle of architectural styles; sad 1970s wallflowers alternate with confident reclaimed warehouses from the nineteenth century; luxurious wharf conversions look up to pseudo-modernist showpieces. The new 'Shard' skyscraper, Europe's tallest office building, towers over the area. 'Shakespeare's Globe', with its circular timber frame construction, naturally stands out in a positive way. The present construction is the love-child of American-born actor Sam Wanamaker, who worked for more than twenty years to get the project done; dying in 1993, he never saw it completed. The theatre we see today opened in 1997; it is clearly a site catering for the culturally-aware tourist. It occupies a spot just over 750 feet (230 metres) away from the site of the original, Elizabethan Globe

Theatre, which was built in 1599 and destroyed by fire in 1613. A replacement, built in 1614, was closed in 1642.

Shakespeare's Globe brings us back to the London of the sixteenth and seventeenth centuries, a London that had changed beyond recognition since the beginning of the Tudor dynasty. By that point it was Europe's largest city, as befits a self-confident trading power with imperialistic ambitions. It was home to a new domestic Christian faith, and also to the greatest literary genius of all time.

All this was still far into the future when Henry VII came to the throne and the name of the ruling family changed from the French Plantagenet to the Welsh Tudor. It was the time when the Middle Ages came to an end. John Wycliffe had translated the Bible into English as early as 1383 and had brought the church to the people – much to the dismay of the Catholic Church. Gutenberg had invented the printing press and just a few years later, William Caxton began to print books in English. The renaissance had started on the continent, and Henry VII brought scholars and artists to England who had a lasting influence on architecture, music and the arts. John Cabot (actually, it was 'Zuan Caboto' – like Columbus, he was Genovese) had sailed west, found new land in today's Canada and named it 'Newfoundland' – a choice of name that aptly reflects the originality of its present inhabitants, if you listen to your friends from Toronto or Montréal.

These were the Tudor years, perhaps best known for their early master of showbiz: Henry VIII – notorious wife-killer and church-founder. When he was crowned in 1509, he had an excellent reputation; he was a brilliant scholar who mastered multiple languages, he was an excellent musician, a powerful athlete and a devout follower of the Catholic Church. Portraits of Henry as a young man show a slim and handsome fellow; nothing like the obese, gout-riddled monster of a man he became in later years.

Henry was the third child of the royal couple, meaning his older brother Arthur was earmarked for succession to the throne. As happened so often in English history, fate had other plans: Arthur died, aged only 15. Henry had to follow him, and in more ways than one. In a brilliant bit of marriage diplomacy, Henry VII had persuaded the Spanish king to let his daughter Catherine join the English heir to the throne in matrimony. This arrangement was simply too good to let it go to waste, just because of the small matter of a death in the family. So, the widow of the deceased young Crown Prince was betrothed to the new, even younger, Crown Prince. Which goes to show that in royal circles marriage is not about love. It is about diplomacy; it is about business; it is about breeding. It also means that 'fun' in a royal's life took place on the side. English royals have been very fond of extramarital activity for centuries, which also means that the scandal-mongering media, who froth at each friendly look Charles or Harry or William cast at any nubile maid, are a bunch of historically uneducated dunderheads.

I mentioned breeding as an important part of a royal

marriage. In fact, it is the most important aspect, and Henry and Catherine did their utmost to produce an heir to the throne. Over the next 24 years, Catherine gave birth to six children – four girls and two sons, and all but one daughter died very early. Henry grew impatient and also desperate: England still smarted from the Wars of the Roses, and he was determined not to allow a tsunami of claims to the throne to be made upon his death. This could only be prevented with a male heir.

We all know what Henry's idea of a solution was – dissolution of the marriage with Catherine of Aragon. It made perfect sense domestically. In the international arena, it was a disaster: one does not simply divorce the Spanish Infanta, particularly at a time when Spain was the world's dominant economic and military power. And you certainly do not do it at a time when Emperor Charles V, Catherine's nephew, held the Pope (who was needed to grant the dissolution) in captivity. As one might have expected, Henry's appeal was denied.

The King's problem had been replaced by a dilemma. As a devout Christian, Henry dared not divorce his wife without the church's say-so. But what do you do if the church won't play along? Well, you set up shop on your own, don't you? Which is exactly what Henry VIII did in 1534 with his 'Act of Supremacy': overnight, the good people of England found themselves no longer Catholic, but C of E. Instead of the pope, a fat king in Hampton Court played second fiddle to the Lord and those who dared to object found themselves to be knocking on the gates of heaven or hell respectively: some 72,000 people who did not want to follow Henry's new outfit were executed.

Surprise: Henry VIII, as head of the new church, dissolved the marriage of the applicant, Henry VIII, and legalised the secret marriage to Anne Boleyn, with whom he had tied the knot a year before. You know what happened over the next few decades: 'divorced, beheaded, died, divorced, beheaded – survived' – that's the little ditty by which one can remember the fates of Henry's six wives.

In the end, there were three surviving children: two daughters (Mary and Elizabeth) and the son Henry had founded the church for, Edward. But Edward was only able to enjoy the crown for a very short time; he died aged 15. Mary and Elizabeth went on to fight for the throne – and it was a bloody fight indeed.

The formation of Henry's new church was one of the most important events in the rise of England as an independent European power. Not because of a theological rift between the island and the continent (it was hardly noticeable), but because England was forced to organise a professional navy to prevent an invasion by the guardian powers of Catholicism, France and Spain. Prior to this, England had not taken much of an interest in seafaring and the navy that existed had largely fallen out of use, since it was no longer needed to ferry knights across the channel to invade some part of France. Henry's navy went on to become the pride of the realm, and it was also the foundation for the imperialist expansion of later years.

If proof were needed for the secular motives behind the founding of the new church, one only need look at Henry's attitude towards doctrine, rites and assets: all possessions of the Catholic Church were confiscated, all monasteries were disestablished. Apart from these structural changes, it was less about reforming the content, than *relabeling* it. If you happened to go into an Anglican service in London, you would not have spotted many differences to Catholic services held in Paris, Rome or Vienna.

The first real push for reform came in the years after Henry's death; young Edward VI, aged nine, acceded to the throne and his advisers used their position to have a go at transforming the church. Their greatest achievement was the introduction of the *Book of Common Prayer*, the first official prayer book in English. When Mary followed her short-lived brother to the throne, these advisers and 300 or so other Protestants received a special reward for their efforts: they were burned at the stake – the Queen's nickname was 'Bloody Mary' and she certainly did her best to earn it. As the only surviving daughter of Catherine of Aragon, Henry VIII's first wife, she felt an obligation to right the wrongs her father had committed, trying hard to reunite the English with the Catholic Church. This set her apart from young Elizabeth, who was duly dispatched to the Tower for allegedly having aided the Protestants. But the reunification was not to be: Mary died after five years on the throne, and Elizabeth I started her own era. It was to last 44 years, quite a good innings for the time.

We have finally reached the 'golden' Elizabethan age, probably the best-spun era in English history. And what fantastic material the spin-doctors had to go about their work with; Elizabeth I, the Virgin Queen. William Shakespeare. Sir Francis Drake. Sir Walter Raleigh. The Spanish Armada. And, of course, London itself, with its never-ending menagerie of thugs and heroes, virtues and vices. Pure cinematic gold, just ask any producer in Hollywood.

Elizabeth I quickly managed to put the vexing issue of the new Church of England to rest: there was to be no going back into the folds of the Roman church and Elizabeth appointed herself 'governor' of the church. Thanks to the growing overseas trade, England blossomed and the new riches spawned a golden age of creativity, which has its most enduring testimony in the works of writers such as William Shakespeare, Christopher Marlowe, Ben Jonson or Edmund Spenser, whose epic poem *The Fairie Queene* is a dazzling homage to the Virgin Queen herself.

Throughout her reign, Elizabeth I faced danger from abroad. As ever, France was just waiting for an opportunity to invade the rich island kingdom, and the Catholic Church gave any such move its blessing – Elizabeth was excommunicated and declared a heretic in 1570. Spain, the other great Catholic power in Europe, was also eager to set foot on the island. While for the French the issue of getting across to England may have been part of the nation's folklore, Spain had quite a few good reasons to be cross with Elizabeth; without the constant support given by the English, the Dutch uprising would have been quelled quickly. Then there were the impertinent attacks on Spanish galleons transporting gold, silver and other treasures from South America. And most of all, the King of Spain (Mary's widower) carried a deep personal grudge: he had proposed marriage to Elizabeth in 1559, only to be cold-shouldered by her. Caramba!

Elizabeth I navigated all these problems with astonishing diplomatic skill but when the greatest threat of all loomed large, she also had amazing luck.

I am, of course, referring to the Spanish Armada, which made its way towards England in 1588. What a sight: 130 ships, equipped with the most modern bits of weaponry available at the time – a mightier fleet had never before sailed the oceans. The Armada first made its way to the Flanders coast to replenish stocks and pick up the Duke of Parma's army for the battles that would ensue once the invasion was under way. One small harbour with 130 big ships huddled in it – the English admiralty could not have believed their luck. Fire ships were directed into the Armada, wreaking havoc and forcing those ships that were still manoeuvrable to take to the North Sea, where they were ravaged by some of the most severe storms ever experienced in those parts. Many ships ran aground along the Irish coast; a last-ditch landing operation in Scotland ended in humiliating defeat. Less than half of the ships that had proudly set sail for England managed to limp back to Spain, and 11,000 mariners died. If you ever hear a Spaniard ranting about the English weather – you will know the reason why.

The Spanish king was not the only nobleman spurned by Elizabeth I. She never married and we could go on speculating as to why this was for hundreds of pages. But we won't. As I said previously, marriage amongst royals was not about love. It was about diplomacy and politics and business. Elizabeth knew this and there were negotiations over many years with many European courts, but they never came to anything. Whichever European aristocrat was selected was bound to drag England into succession squabbles. An English aristocrat was out of the question as well; domestic envy would inevitably lead to domestic strife. When it became clear that Elizabeth would not produce an heir to the throne, her advisers beseeched her to clarify the question of succession – to no avail; the Queen simply refused to talk about the matter. Behind her back, negotiations commenced with James VI, King of Scotland. His feelings towards Elizabeth were very clear: he was the son of Mary, Queen of Scots, who had been driven from Scotland for her Catholic faith to be kept under arrest in England for the rest of her life; she was executed in 1587.

It must have been a special triumph for James to ascend the English throne, which he did in 1603, as James I. Just a year later, and much against the will of both the English and Scottish parliaments, he declared himself King of Great Britain, but the two kingdoms formally remained separate for another 100 years.

The Elizabethan Age is seen as a golden one, very much due to the glorious figure of William Shakespeare. But Shakespeare was just one of many actors, writers and theatre managers who fought for commercial success in the capital. Historically, the lasting establishment of the Church of England is of much higher significance. Economically, the ventures into piracy, colonialism and slavery brought massive fortunes. Francis Drake had circumnavigated the world in 1577 and arrived home laden with the bounties of the Spanish ports in South America. His expeditions, and those of his fellow buccaneers, filled the royal coffers with untold riches; just one successful expedition could be worth a year's domestic tax revenue.

Elizabeth I, who knew her Latin, would probably have said *pecunia non olet*, money doesn't smell. From 1584, the English ran their first American colony in Virginia, which produced potatoes and tobacco – and cotton, of course, but that became important some years later. Since the mid-1560s, Elizabeth I had invested in the triangular trade, which delivered slaves to the Americas. The profit brought in by these expeditions: 60 per cent. *Non olet*, indeed.

Oh, and two of the most important accomplishments in human history were introduced in this glorious age. The first one comes to us thanks to the genius of Robert Recorde, a humble Welshman who wrote educational books for children. He invented the 'equals' sign, the humble but brilliantly elegant '=' which makes mathematics so much more palatable.

And Sir John Harrington, godson of Elizabeth I, re-invented what had been forgotten since Roman times; in 1592 Elizabeth gracefully premiered the flushing water toilet.

We have embarked upon this chapter with a walk across the Thames towards Southwark and the reproduction of Shakespeare's Globe Theatre. So, let's talk about the Bard.

It is not easy to describe the influence Shakespeare had, and still has, in the world of art. As well as dramatics and literature, all the other art forms have also embraced his work: music and dance, painting and sculpture. Today, the world celebrates 'World Book Day' on April 23, the day of Shakespeare's birth in 1564 and also of his death, in 1616. The body of his work is of average bulk: 38 plays, 154 sonnets, two long poems and a couple of shorter ones. Even in the twenty-first century, he is the playwright most often staged throughout the world, which obviously shows that his dramatic art still touches audiences some 400 years later.

We do not know too much about Shakespeare's life. The church register in Stratford-upon-Avon records his birth and death and his marriage to an older woman in the mid-1580s. We find him in London in 1590, where he joins a theatre troupe – but we don't know whether this was as an actor or a writer or just a general dogsbody. There is a bad review of his theatrical work in 1592, and as every artist knows, you have only made it when the bad reviews start coming in; it means that you are taken seriously.

Around this time he became co-owner of London's leading troupe, the 'Lord Chamberlain's Men', named in honour of their aristocratic patron. Such patronage was mandatory to be granted a licence; after Elizabeth's death, Shakespeare's troupe received the highest possible patronage and duly changed their name to 'The King's Men'.

We do not know what Shakespeare looked like, nor whether he was a closet Catholic. Similarly, we don't have a clue whether he loved only women or whether he took the odd fancy to a young man (some of his sonnets are clearly addressed to a man). And we cannot be certain whether he wrote all of his texts himself. Every now and then, doubts are raised as to the true authorship of Shakespeare's plays. Christopher Marlowe, Francis Bacon or Edward de Vere are all touted as possible alternatives. This may or may not be true, but it would have been against the artistic practice of Shakespeare's day if he had shunned collaboration with other writers. Although today we perceive his works as a beacon of art, their creation back then would have resembled the processes we find among the teams of script writers toiling in one of today's soap opera sweatshops. Shakespeare borrowed myths and mysteries, plundered plays from all ages (classics as well as Italian *Commedia dell'arte*) and he let himself be 'inspired' by rivals' texts as well. This may sound shocking, but taking other people's ideas and using them to one's own benefit was customary at the time. As Alexander Pope put it so elegantly a century later in his 'Essay on Criticism': 'True wit is nature to advantage dressed / What oft was thought but ne'er so well expressed.'

Shakespeare's career had its highlights, and he commanded professional fame amongst his peers and moderate wealth in his lifetime. But his reputation reached the giddy heights on which it rests today only in the late eighteenth century, when *Hamlet* became a seminal text for the Romantic Movement all over Europe.

Most of Shakespeare's work was produced between 1590 and 1613; the first definitive collection, the 'First Folio' with 36 plays, was published in 1623. Shakespeare's early plays convey a good education; he picks up the classical themes and stories that were part of the curriculum in the grammar schools of the time. Given that Shakespeare's career began during Elizabeth's reign, we should not be surprised to see him describe the advent of the Tudors as the beginning of a golden age. Bad leadership stands out as the cause of misery in his History Plays, with a weak king, such as Richard II, and an evil monster, such as Richard III, demonstrating the polar extremes of bad leadership.

Dating Shakespeare's plays is not too easy. The general consensus today is that the History Plays, starting with *Richard II*, belong in his earliest period. From 1595, there were tragedies, such as *Julius Caesar* and *Romeo and Juliet*, as well as comedies like *A Midsummer Night's Dream*. The great tragedies, including *Macbeth* and *Hamlet*, were produced from 1600 onwards; 'tragicomedies', such as *The Tempest* belong to the latest period, post-1608. When we look at his writing, we notice the gradual development of his style: while he adhered to convention and a rather high level of expression in the early plays, he relaxes the formalities as he becomes more confident as a writer and plays with convention. Towards the end of his career, his writing freely mixes various levels of formality and expression, allowing his characters to develop into true individuals.

Do you admire actors such as Ralph Richardson or Laurence Olivier, with their clipped deliverance of Shakespeare's words? Well, the words may well be Shakespeare's but he probably would not have understood them, because in his time, pronunciation was quite different. In fact, Shakespeare's own pronunciation would probably have been close to what we would perceive as an American accent. The British Library has recently issued a recording that uses the original pronunciation – it is well worth listening to.*

William Shakespeare earned enough money from his endeavours to buy a large house in Stratford-upon-Avon. Upon his death, he bequeathed his possessions to his children. His wife got the 'second best bed'. Despite his modest wealth and artistic fame, his contemporaries would certainly have treated Shakespeare just as they treated all the other acting folk – with disdain. In Elizabethan England, theatres were not temples to Apollo, but rough dens of entertainment and iniquity. This is

---

* Shakespeare's Original Pronunciation. Speeches and scenes performed as Shakespeare would have heard them. London, 2012.

the reason why The Globe, and many other theatres, were built on the south bank of the river: it was beyond the reach of the city authorities.

Shakespeare's life spanned the 'golden years' of Elizabeth's reign and the early years of the Stuarts.

What a difference a king makes.

Ely, Cambridgeshire

*Trouble and strife; a plot and a king's head –
apart from that, not much fun*

The charming historic city of Ely, home to one of the most magnificent cathedrals in England, is our next destination. Nestled in the countryside near Cambridge, one would not think that this tranquil little city was home to one of the greatest and most controversial characters in English history – Oliver Cromwell. Even today, mentioning his name may well terminate polite small talk. Many people see him as a reformer who laid the foundations for modern governance and religious freedoms; but to others, he is an odious Puritan hypocrite who used extreme violence to fulfil his ambitions. Friends and foes alike will concede that he was indeed a very important person; only Queen Victoria has more streets named after her in today's England.

Ely is dominated by its splendid cathedral, which is one of the most beautiful buildings the country has to offer. Its famous octagonal dome is a marvel of architecture, especially when you remember that it was built in the fourteenth century, when construction technology still had some way to go, particularly when it came to the stability of roof constructions.

The city also provides us with a beautifully reconstructed Tudor-era house in which Oliver Cromwell lived from 1636 to 1646 and which had come into his possession upon the death of his uncle, who also bequeathed to him the position of local tax collector. Cromwell was also a governor of the Thomas Parson's Charity, which is still active today, providing grants and housing to needy locals. Here, in deepest East Anglia, was the military and spiritual foundation for his rise to power.

But we are getting ahead of ourselves once more. England had just found a new king, James VI of Scotland, who combined his duties in Edinburgh with his new job in London, where he was now known as James I. His accession to the throne was due to a parliamentary committee, which had been tasked with finding a credible successor to the childless Queen Elizabeth I. As we know today, a camel is a horse designed by a committee – and the decision in favour of James is right up there with the other big daft decisions that changed world history.

It might have been a good idea for the Honourable Members of Parliament to read James's books – because this was a king who was not only educated but also very eager to put his thoughts in writing. If they had done that, they would have noticed that James was possessed with the belief that a monarch has a duty only to God and not to secular institutions. This may have been interesting stuff for a debate at a university, but it was far from the political reality of the time. Elizabeth's reign had seen the emergence of a new and powerful class of society: the merchants and investors who really ran the country's economy, bestrode the political stage with confidence and demanded a greater say in the governing of the realm.

Under these circumstances, appointing James I was as clever as hiring a footballer with an allergy to grass. But here we are, with the first in the succession of the Stuart monarchs – there were only five, and they were a disaster. One caused a civil war and ended up with his head cut off; another one got kicked out of the country. And James is to blame for a good part of the mayhem. First, he had himself acknowledged by an act of parliament, which seemed to be a good move. It wasn't; parliament understood the act as a reassurance and acceptance of its constitutional powers – in the end it served as one of the grounds on which Charles I was tried and executed half a century later.

James's second move was not much better: he officially declared his intention to unify the two kingdoms of England and Scotland, which the parliaments in London and Edinburgh swiftly rebuffed. Rumours spread that he intended to reinstate the Catholic Church in England and his diplomatic success in ending the war with Spain, which had been going on since the days of the Armada, only served as proof: if somebody had such a good rapport with the papists, he must be up to something, mustn't he?

But James did not launch a comeback for Catholicism in England. In fact, after two Catholic-led plots against his life were discovered and thwarted, he ordered all Jesuits and Catholic clergy to leave the country. Such strong anti-Catholic actions led to the event which is still celebrated to this day with bonfires and fireworks: the Gunpowder Plot.

> Remember, remember the fifth of November,
> gunpowder, treason and plot,
> I see no reason why gunpowder treason
> should ever be forgot.
> Guy Fawkes, Guy Fawkes,
> 'twas his intent
> to blow up the King and the Parliament.
> Three score barrels of powder below,
> Poor old England to overthrow:
> By God's providence he was catch'd
> With a dark lantern and burning match.
> Holloa boys, holloa boys, make the bells ring.
> Holloa boys, holloa boys, God save the King!
> Hip hip hoorah!

This merry song gives a short impression of what happened. A group of disappointed Catholics picked the day of the ceremonial opening of parliament on 5 November 1605, to blow up the building and everyone in attendance. Being proper English gentlemen, the plotters sent a letter to a perceived ally, the Catholic Baron Monteagle, warning him not to attend the opening; the noble Lord proved his nobility by duly handing over the document to justice officials. A search party found Guy Fawkes guarding 36 barrels of gun powder in the cellars underneath the chamber – if he had succeeded, the whole building would have been reduced to rubble and King, Lords and Members of parliament would have formed an orderly queue at heaven's gate (or at the entry to the 'other place', as it may be). As we know, Guy Fawkes did not succeed, and his effigies are still burnt today, probably in homage to the punishment meted out to the plotters; it was nasty. First, the men were drawn along the ground behind a horse to the place of execution; then hanged until they were unconscious; then disembowled, and finally the corpses were cut into four pieces. Londoners found this kind of entertainment exhilarating. Happy days!

One might have thought that this affair would have brought King and parliament closer together. It didn't. For the next twenty years, both parties went at each other's throats with great enthusiasm whenever there was an opportunity. The King wants to levy taxes – let's block it! The parliament is blocking my tax proposals? Let's dissolve it! For many years, James governed without a sitting parliament, leaving behind a deeply divided country when he died in 1625. Ardent royalists were pitted against the ever more radical faction of Protestants who would not agree to the King's ideas of the world and the religious conformity these ideas demanded. The Pilgrim Fathers' journey to America in 1620 was a result of this conflict.

The new king, Charles I, was unfortunate in many ways.

Unfortunate for succeeding a father who had poisoned relations with parliament; unfortunate for sharing his father's thinking as to the role of the monarch; unfortunate for marrying a French Catholic princess; unfortunate for having the Thirty Years' War ravaging continental Europe and radicalising the religious conflicts; unfortunate for being surrounded by advisers who strongly opposed Calvinism; unfortunate for lacking the intelligence to smother parliamentary dissent, and unfortunate, of course, for losing his head in the end.

Charles had inherited his father's talent for losing friends and alienating people, especially when it came to money matters. Parliament tried to put things on a sustainable footing for public coffers by rejecting Charles's demands and even pushing through the 'Petition of Rights' in 1628, which gave budgetary control to parliament and granted civil liberties. But these restraints only served to make Charles and his advisers ever more ingenious: to raise money, they dug out an ancient law that ordered every Englishman earning more than £40 per year to be present at the king's coronation. The law was 350 years old and had not been observed for centuries but it was very useful; everyone who had not turned up for the coronation was made to pay up.

Charles dissolved the parliament in 1629 and reigned without it for over a decade. What may have looked like a good idea at the time, turned out to be a crucial part of the King's undoing: remote from the political debate, neither he nor his advisers noticed the shifting sentiment amongst his subjects, who grew more and more radically opposed to his policies. When parliament was recalled, the opposition to the King was overwhelming. True to form, in 1642 Charles headed a troop of guardsmen to enter the Commons chamber in order to arrest five obstreperous Members of Parliament; and true to form, he ended up with egg on his face. The five culprits had done a runner, and the Speaker of the House enforced parliamentary privilege by refusing to answer the King's questions as to their whereabouts. Despite failing, his arrogant act was the last straw for parliament; open warfare was now unavoidable. And no English monarch has set foot in the Commons since then, which is why the annual State Opening of Parliament takes place in the Lords and still entails a rigmarole of customs, which include a member of the Commons being held hostage at Buckingham Palace during the ceremony.

The Civil War that followed lasted three years and Charles had to admit defeat in the end. Ever the diplomat, he never considered giving in to his opponents, who now demanded a constitutional monarchy. Having fled from captivity, he gathered loyalists in Scotland and a second bout of warfare ravaged the country from 1648. Charles lost again and this time, parliament were not taking any chances. Charles I was not the first king in English history to be deposed and executed; but the king who would not accept any authority other than God was the only monarch to be tried by the citizens he despised, found guilty of treason and beheaded, in 1649. A likeness of his head can be seen on the wall of Westminster

Abbey, gazing across the road upon the statue of his nemesis – Oliver Cromwell.

Cromwell was not a handsome man. Contemporary portraits (which, one can assume, tried to flatter their subject) depict a burly John Bull. His demeanour gives meaning to the old saying that with some people, you do not need to know them to abhor them – instant loathing can save so much time. To many people, Cromwell is the arch-spoiler of sports; with his government came the prohibition of almost anything that people found nice or pleasant. Music, theatre and dancing were out. Horse racing and fox hunting were next to face the chop – both were perceived as pastimes for idle aristocrats, whom Cromwell's Puritans despised. You will even hear that Christmas was cancelled, as it provided opportunity for joyful revelries; well, not quite – Christmas remained in place but minus the decorations and the food and obviously, the office parties.

So, everybody had a really dreary time. Are you honestly surprised when I tell you that Cromwell himself led a lavish lifestyle while in power, with wine and food and a personal organist to provide the entertainment? He would have made a great evangelical pastor in today's USA!

Oliver Cromwell hailed from 'salt of the earth' country squire stock; as a young man he made a name for himself as a rabble-rouser, as did most of his ilk. Chasing skirt and getting drunk were his major activities during his days at Cambridge University, and he found himself barred from many a tavern.

He sobered up somewhat during his time as a Member of Parliament, where he strongly opposed the shenanigans of Charles I and, along with many other members, joined the ranks of the radical Puritans. At the outbreak of the Civil War, Cromwell set up his own troops and shortly after was named Commander-in-Chief of all parliamentary troops, known as 'the Roundheads'. His success as a military leader was mainly due to his loyal 'New Model Army', which revolutionised military culture. Officers were elected by the soldiers and it was their duty to lead their men not only in battle, but also in prayer. This new approach instilled a sense of togetherness amongst the troops, which gave them a huge psychological advantage over their adversaries, 'the Cavaliers'.

Parliament took charge of government after the fall of Charles I. It swiftly deposed all the bishops in the Anglican Church and declared religious freedom… except for Catholics. This strengthened the religious sects that had been around for quite a while by then, and with religious extremism came a number of unorthodox political movements. There were the 'Ranters', who demanded that people should be allowed to do whatever they wanted to, including indulging in alcohol, dancing and sex, because all these pleasures had been instilled in man by God – and how could God's creatures commit a sin? The 'Levellers' demanded equal suffrage for all men, irrespective of their possessions; the 'Diggers' dreamt of a proto-communist society with communal possession of everything and equality of men and women. Shock! Horror!

Cromwell, the radical, found himself on the conservative end of politics and, in 1653, dissolved parliament. He took over government as 'Lord Protector' of the new 'Commonwealth' – a king by any other name.

It was in Ireland where Cromwell imposed the new set of regulations with particular rigour: the army was set upon the Irish, officially to quell Catholic resistance to the new regime, but really it was more of a land-grabbing exercise for Cromwell's cronies. Thousands of Irish were driven from their properties and the army did not make time for legal arguments: those who resisted were killed or driven to emigrate. Cromwell's boys were particularly fond of razors, which they used to slash the faces of uncooperative natives. The consequences of Cromwell's Irish expedition were tragic: more than a million people died of famine and disease; less than half of the population survived. I mentioned previously that in England, only Queen Victoria has more streets named after her than Cromwell; in Ireland he does not have a single one.

Cromwell's government is rightly remembered as a time of mirthless ardour and criminal mistreatment of those who got in his way. But the Commonwealth also brought religious tolerance to England (except for Catholics). Before Cromwell, everybody had to be a member of the Church of England and failure to attend church in one's home parish was penalised. Now, whoever wanted to break away was allowed to do so, and numerous sects sprang up in a short time. Cromwell's era also saw the official return of Jews to England, who had been banned for almost 350 years. The first English translation of the Quran was also published in those years.

Following Cromwell's death in 1658, his son Richard took over – the republic had decayed into a dynastic fiefdom. But Richard did not possess his father's ruthless cunning and intelligence, and the army leadership swiftly got rid of him. Which left the question, who to turn to next? Well, it looks as if this set of Puritans had an almost Python-esque sense of humour (or someone must have organised a gigantic piss-up): they called upon the beheaded king's son, who had spent the duration of the Commonwealth exiled in France.

This was 1660, the Restoration period began; the monarchy returned, theatres were re-opened and everybody got busy having a very good time. Charles II and his merry henchmen took revenge upon those who had done for daddy – those signatories of the death warrant that were still alive were now tried and executed themselves. Oliver Cromwell's body was exhumed, sentenced to death in a show trial and decapitated. His head was stuck on a pole and displayed for twenty years, until a gust of wind blew it down. Isn't life great?

Had the new Stuart king learnt anything from the fate of his father? Of course not! Kings are not selected for their brain cells. Charles II continued the feuds about money and privileges and religion that his father and grandfather had indulged in. And when this Charles died without a legitimate heir (despite having sired twelve illegitimate children through extra-curricular activity, both Diana and Camilla are direct descendants), his brother James II – a Catholic – continued the family tradition of acting like a prat. Again, parliament got to its feet, this time not for a Civil War but to kick the King out of the country and install his daughter Mary, along with her husband William of Orange (who had assembled a large invasion army, just in case), as joint successors. They called it 'the Glorious Revolution', and the year was 1688.

Eyam, Derbyshire

Plague and fire; and a grand new cathedral

Apart from the endless squabbles between the kings and parliament, the Restoration period saw two major disasters and the emergence of one of the great geniuses of world history. The first disaster was the Great Plague that struck in 1665, which killed off nearly a third of London's population and untold numbers in the rest of the country. The second disaster was the Great Fire that ravaged London in 1666. And the Great Genius was Isaac Newton.

The plague had come to England from time to time ever since 1348; the Great Plague was the fourth recorded outbreak in the seventeenth century alone. It was concentrated in London; everyone who could afford it left town to be safe from the disease. This seems to have been the thinking that brought the plague to the idyllic town of Eyam in Derbyshire: a box of clothes sent from London is said to have carried the virus. The disease spread quickly and the inhabitants were faced with a difficult choice: abandon the town and risk spreading the disease throughout the Peak District, or stay put, look after those affected by the plague and give them a decent burial.

Led by their two parsons, the good people of Eyam chose the latter, shut themselves off from the world for about a year and turned the place into a huge plague house. People from neighbouring villages and estates left food outside the town, grateful for the heroic gesture. The gesture was not an empty one: the plague stayed within Eyam and did not affect the rest of the county. It is assumed that around two thirds of Eyam's population lost their lives, although the exact figure will probably remain unknown.

With today's science we know that stringent hygiene might have prevented the virus from spreading; actually by staying together in a closely confined area, the people of Eyam created an ideal habitat for rats and their fleas that carry the plague. But this does not diminish the gesture of the village that chose to die. Every year on the last Sunday in August, there is an open-air service to honour the people of Eyam. It is well worth attending and paying homage.

Just as with the Great Plague, the Great Fire of 1666 was not unique as such – in the seventeenth century there were six large fires in London alone. But this one was different: it destroyed 13,000 houses, 87 churches, and 44 guild halls. Most Londoners fled to the suburbs; the two neighbouring villages of Highbury and Islington alone sheltered some 200,000 people.

Famously, the fire started on 2 September 1666, at around 2 p.m. in Thomas Farynor's bakery in Pudding Lane, just a stone's throw away from the present site of the Bank of

England. What actually caused the initial fire is unknown and it doesn't really matter, because disaster struck when the tar barrels in Farynor's cellar exploded and set alight the hay stacked in the yard of the inn next door. The fire brigade arrived about an hour later, headed by the mayor, Sir Thomas Bloodworth, who gave his expert comment: 'A woman might piss it out!' he said and went back to sleep.

Well, English humour doesn't always come in the most constructive ways, and this is a prime example of the wrong joke at the wrong time. If you had planned an insurance scam, this would have been the method of choice to get your fire burning: it had been a long, hot and dry summer, and the timber framed houses burnt like tinder. Within hours, the fire reached the docks along the Thames, which were stacked to the rafters with oil, coal, tallow and other flammable materials. They went 'boom' and the smouldering debris spread the fire even further. To make the situation worse, most home owners refused permission to have their houses torn down in order to create firebreaks. Invaluable time, houses and lives were lost until these firebreaks were at last created by royal decree. Charles II also ordered any military personnel he could lay his hands on to assist in fighting the fire, and both the King and his brother James were spotted toiling away tirelessly with shovels and buckets to keep the disaster at bay.

It took more than three days before the fire came under control, and the blaze could be seen from as far away as Oxford; it took weeks before the ruins had cooled down sufficiently to get the clean up and repair going. As always with disasters like this, people quickly began looking for somebody to blame. How could a simple accident in a bakery explain a disaster on such a scale? Well, there was the time-honoured scapegoat: blame the papists. It worked. A hapless French watchmaker, Robert 'Lucky' Huber, who had arrived in London two days after the fire began, confessed his guilt and was hanged. And for the next 200 years, a plaque at the Monument reminded passers-by of the fiendish Popish plot.

Apart from looters and phoney evangelists, there is another profession which greatly appreciates destroyed cityscapes: architects. They call it a 'clean canvass' and set about planning the future. Christopher Wren did just this and proposed a modern new city with wide avenues and houses built of stone. Londoners disliked the idea and insisted on reconstructing the city along the traditional street pattern – and this is why, to this day, the City of London consists of a warren of alleyways and little, cramped streets. But Wren was allowed to build St. Paul's Cathedral. So, something good did come out of it eventually.

Grantham, Lincolnshire

Where we learn about Calculus
but we don't have to do the maths

When London burnt, Isaac Newton was far away and blissfully unaware of his imminent discoveries and fame. Or, as one might say, the apple had not yet dropped.

Newton ranks among the most important scientists of all time; his groundbreaking discoveries in mathematics, optics, mechanics and astronomy set the scene far into the twentieth century, when Max Planck and Albert Einstein were the first to develop his findings in decisive ways. He was born in humble circumstances and was raised by his grandmother. He excelled at school in Grantham (the Lincolnshire town where Margaret Thatcher grew up) and was awarded a scholarship to Cambridge, where he read mathematics and physics without making too much of an impact. The plague that befell England in 1665 set him onto his career: when the university closed to avoid the epidemic, Newton returned home and, not having much to do, worked himself into a creative frenzy. When he returned to Cambridge in 1667, he had done the preparatory work for a number of novel theories, from optics to calculus, which he developed simultaneously to, but independent of, German scholar, Gottfried Leibnitz. In 1669, he became Professor of Mathematics and was accorded a rare exception by the university: in those days, university teachers had to be ordained clerics within the Church of England. Newton was spared this task, which may have been of even greater benefit to his prospective parishioners – a genius he may have been, but his lectures were notorious for being as boring as watching paint dry; students deserted him in droves.

The fruits of Newton's research were much juicier than his lectures: his *Philosphiae Naturalis Principia Mathematica*, published in 1687, paved the way for new discoveries in engineering; without his findings, the Industrial Revolution could not possibly have unfolded in the way that it did. Newton's obscure hobbies are less well known: roughly half of his writing is concerned with Christian mysticism and with alchemy. When he died, his body showed enormous levels of mercury, which he used in his efforts to extract gold from whatever material he could lay his hands on.

Newton's reputation outshone his contemporaries even during his lifetime. He did not face much opposition when he decided to become a Member of Parliament, where his main contribution seems to have been complaints about the draught in the chamber. In 1696, he took over the governorship of the Royal Mint, which his predecessors had perceived as a well-paid quango. Newton took his job seriously, hunting down counterfeiters and establishing the Gold Standard for the pound. This achievement alone would have secured him a place in history, as it would prove to be the foundation for England's economic success over the next centuries.

Great men don't need to make friends, and Newton seems to have been extremely talented at not making friends. Just think of the epic dispute with Leibniz over calculus, or his embittered opposition to John Harrison, who solved the problem of calculating longitude. But Harrison was only a clockmaker without a university education, and the great Newton was simply not big enough to afford him the respect he deserved.

Sir Isaac Newton died in 1727. Alexander Pope's epitaph is perhaps the most beautiful tribute ever to have been paid to a scientist:

'Nature and nature's laws lay hid in night
God said: "Let Newton be!" and all was light.'

The City of London

We come across bubble trouble and some Georges

The times, they were a-changing, to paraphrase Bob Dylan: with the coronation of Mary and William III, parliament had stated once and for all that the era of divine authority was over for the English monarchy. The balance of power tilted towards those who called the shots in everyday life – rural agricultural magnates, merchants and the emerging species of industrialists, with their representatives in parliament, the 'Whigs' and the 'Tories' (named after Irish bandits). It was the north of England that was the epicentre of the social upheaval which accompanied the changes. The monarchs signed the 'Bill of Rights', another document that granted rights to the public and took privileges away from the royals. The bill ruled that the king could not levy taxes or pass legislation without parliamentary consent and that he could not have a standing army in peace time. The Act of Settlement ruled that no Catholic could ever accede to the English throne and that the monarch could not marry a Catholic – these stipulations are still in force today, although it now looks as if the current government might get round to getting rid of them. The heads of state of the Commonwealth have already agreed that Catholics are no longer such a danger, so Prince William's offspring might now be allowed to cast an eye in that direction.

The deposed king, James II (Mary's father), tried to win back his power by force, assembling troops first in Scotland, then in Ireland. In both cases he was defeated by the English troops and even humiliatingly forced to abandon his soldiers in Ireland, which earned him the lovely nickname 'James the be-shitten'. Irish Protestants still wear William III's orange colours with pride during the annual 'Marching Season'. This lovely tradition is unfailingly accompanied by the pleasant Irish sport of bashing each other's heads in.

As both William and Mary were quite young when they came to the throne, it was hoped that they would produce an heir in due time. They didn't. When Mary died, parliament's hopes rested upon the next in line, Mary's younger sister Anne. Whilst William ruled on, Anne did her utmost to comply, becoming pregnant no fewer than nineteen times and giving birth to five children. Four of them died as infants, the fifth only reached the tender age of eleven. When William III died in 1702, succumbing to injuries he sustained when his horse stumbled over a mole hill, the allies of the young Prince James, who had been pipped to the throne by his sisters (Mary and then Anne) and lived in exile in France, toasted 'the little gentleman in the black coat'.

Anne took over, the last of the Stuarts, although it had been clear for a while that she would not be able to produce an heir.

Horrified, parliament had already begun to take a close look at those in line to the throne. Horror turned into desperation and then into farce: the 57 people closest to the throne were *all* Catholics. The 'Act of Settlement' had been passed in 1701, a year before Anne became queen, and so number 58, the first Protestant in line, was told to put her towel on the royal deck chair: Sophia, Electress of Hanover, a granddaughter of James I.

And thus the nationality of the English monarchs changed for the last time. Since the Romans left, the English throne had been occupied by various Germans, Danish and Norwegians, followed by French, Welsh and Scottish kings. Now the Germans came back, and they have held on to the throne ever since.

When a law is passed named the 'Act of Settlement' you may be excused for thinking that this actually settles a certain matter. In this case, it didn't: the Scots, who had provided England with shared monarchs for a century (only to see most of them beheaded or driven out of the country), found the idea of cheering an imported German king not as enticing as the English thought they would. As politics goes, a great big tussle started, which saw the English in the better position. The 'Alien Act' was passed in 1705, which declared every Scotsman to be an alien in England and forbade the import of coal, wool, cattle and other goods. Daniel Defoe, whose *Robinson Crusoe* would later become one of the seminal texts of world literature, wrote in exasperation: 'Never two nations, that had so much affinity in circumstances, have had such inveteracy and aversion to one another in their blood.'

We cannot know whether Scottish resistance was a gesture by a proud nation or a canny negotiating trick by politicians who saw the writing on the wall: after much wrangling, the two parliaments agreed upon the 'Act of Union' in 1707, which created a unified kingdom with a common flag (the Union Jack), a single parliament in Westminster (which was expanded to accommodate Scottish MPs and peers), a single currency and standard English measurements. Scotland retained some of its own legislative powers, its judiciary and the Presbyterian *Kirk*, which is quite distinct from the Church of England. These sovereign powers have remained with Scotland ever since and the devolved parliament, which was introduced in 1997, has not diminished this position. In late 2011, Alex Salmond, Scotland's nationalist First Minister, announced plans for a referendum to split up the union saying that a separate Scotland 'speaks with its own voice, stands taller in the world and takes responsibility for its own future'. Sounds nice – but what's the big difference? one is tempted to ask, and even the Scots have not reacted too enthusiastically.

So, when Anne finally met her maker in 1714, England became a province of the mighty kingdom of Hanover. Sophia herself had died just two months before she would have taken the throne and so it was her son, George, who entered London in full pomp and circumstance; it took 260 carriages to transport his entourage through the bustling streets of the world's largest city. 'German George' did not find England too attractive; he never learnt English and skived off to Hanover whenever he could. The little business of government was handed over to a trusted adviser: Sir Robert Walpole, who effectively became the United Kingdom's first prime minister, although that post was not officially created. One wonders how master and minister communicated. Both had a little French and a bit of Latin. Well, it didn't hurt the country to have a monarch without too much ambition.

I mentioned earlier that the real powers of modern society had taken over some political powers as well. Since Sir Isaac Newton had imposed the gold standard for the pound, England's financial sector had become even more important. In the early eighteenth century, with well-established foreign trading structures and the industrial revolution getting in gear (once again thanks to Newton, whose work on dynamics and mechanics provided the basis for many inventions in engineering), the future seemed golden. But, as every good Puritan will tell you; when something seems too good to be true, it usually is.

England had known stock-holding companies for a long time; they were used to finance trade ventures and colonial expansion. The Bank of England had opened for business in 1694 and had started a thriving trade in government bonds. Investors loved it, and bond-financing became all the rage for public as well as private ventures. In 1711, the South Sea Company was founded, which sold bonds to finance the slave trade and other businesses. In time-honoured tradition, the swift success of the South Sea Company fostered a flurry of copy-cat ventures – one even went by the wonderful moniker

'A Company for Carrying Out an Undertaking of Great Advantage, but Nobody to Know What it is'.

The mother of all financial market bubbles began to balloon, and of course, it ended in tears. The proprietors of the South Sea Company had obviously acquired their skills at some precursor of the Lehman Brothers School of Finance: at the height of the boom, 1720, the company held a third of all existing government bonds and within weeks, the price of its stocks rose eightfold. And then it crashed back to its original price. Never in the history of England had there been so many bankruptcies; huge swathes of the financial industry were destroyed. There wasn't even a scrappage programme for second-hand horse carriages, and it did not dawn upon Walpole's government that it might be a God-given duty to bail out troubled banks and financial institutions. So, those who had taken part in the get-rich-quick scheme really had to bear the brunt. Isn't it nice that times have changed since then?

Since that time, the City of London has been synonymous with the financial industry. Back then, deals were done mostly in the area's coffee houses; even today the people employed to manage the building at Lloyd's are still called 'waiters'.

Apart from the little issue of the world's first stock exchange disaster, the first three Georges did well for England. Well, they lost most of the American colonies, but we won't dwell on that little mishap. Despite the South Sea Bubble hiccup, the country continued to prosper, the industrialisation of mining, agriculture and textile production led to huge increases in productivity. The freedoms granted in the Bill of Rights made England a haven for political discourse and radical pamphleteering; freedom of the press had been granted in 1695, and a copyright bill had been passed in 1710.

The new elites also inspired the arts: in literature, writers such as Daniel Defoe, Henry Fielding and Samuel Richardson created the modern novel; Dr Johnson compiled the first English dictionary. Acidic satire was adored by the new bourgeois class, which revelled in the unmasking of corruption and vanity. Alexander Pope and Jonathan Swift were the literary masters of this genre. William Hogarth's graphic works portrayed a society in radical change with acerbic wit and irony. Joshua Reynolds and Thomas Gainsborough created a decidedly English school of painting; the landscaper 'Capability' Brown developed the 'English Garden', which contrasted Italian and French formalism with a new concept of beauty that left nature seemingly untouched. Periodical magazines and newspapers flourished; in 1785, the *Daily Universal Register* was started, which was renamed three years later and became *The Times*. James Watt developed the first steam engine that could be used in industry, James Cook sailed to Australia and even England's wars went well: France lost huge swaths of land to England in India and North America in the Seven Years War, which was fought on battlefields in Europe, Asia and America, making it the first real 'World War'.

We don't need bother too much with the shenanigans of the individual Georges – of course there was intrigue and ambition, squabbles about taxes and status. Perhaps the most memorable thing about these kings was the 'madness' of King George III, who oversaw the defeat in the American War of Independence, as well as the first bout of the Napoleonic wars. He suffered from porphyria, a rare enzyme disorder that can lead to severe mental problems. In 1810, parliament installed the next George as Prince Regent.

When George IV finally ascended to the throne in 1820, he had already solidly ruined his reputation. He loved luxury and indulged in all sorts of excesses. His contemporaries described him as being extremely obese in stature and completely egotistical in mind. He loved the company of eccentric artists, architects and hangers-on, such as the infamous Beau Brummel, the daddy of all dandies. His legacy is impressive: look at Regent's Street and Regent's Park in London or savour the folly of the Brighton Pavilion – that was what George IV liked. Parliament had to bail him out more than once; the King had no time for little things such as paying debts. His subjects loathed him and when he died in 1830, *The Times* did not hold back from expressing the nation's sentiments:

There never was an individual less regretted by his fellow-creatures than this deceased king. What eye has wept for him? What heart has heaved one throb of unmercenary sorrow?... If he ever had a friend – a devoted friend in any rank of life – we protest that the name of him or her never reached us.

Oh, and that was a friendly write-up.

Apart from dubious would-be artists, the regency period also had a superstar: George Gordon Lord Byron, the most popular poet of his time. He was a genuine pop star, breaking the hearts of many a young lass (and lad). He also wrote one of my favourite political poems, about Lord Castlereagh, the minister in charge of the forces who had crushed a peaceful workers' protest in Manchester in 1819, the 'Peterloo Massacre'. Castlereagh later committed suicide, and Byron honoured his memory thus:

> Posterity will ne'er survey
> A nobler grave than this:
> Here lie the bones of Castlereagh:
> Stop, traveller, and piss.

Despite all his dallying with various maidens, George IV did not provide a legitimate heir; his only daughter having died at a young age. Brother William stepped up to the plate, but he too could only serve as a stop-gap. William, who had never expected to become king, had led a jolly life as a sailor and man-about-town. He had cohabited with Mrs Jordan, an actress, for twenty years, and together they had ten children. None of them could lay a claim to the throne – if that had been different, the present British Prime Minister, David Cameron, would have a genuine claim. But it wasn't, so he doesn't.

Manchester, Greater Manchester

Where Jennies spin trouble;
and martyrs and a king called Ludd

But a good time was not had by all. In the north of England, the Georgian period saw a rapid growth in industry, fuelled by the new technologies and the riches derived from the triangular trade. Especially around Manchester, these developments hit home. The industrialisation of many parts of the economy caused an upheaval of the traditional work patterns and ways to earn a living. Farmers on smallholdings had no chance of competing with the new agricultural industrialists; many had to abandon their farms and migrated to the cities to seek a job in the new factories. There, they had to deal with things like the 'Spinning Jenny', which was introduced in 1764. It operated up to 120 spools at once to produce yarn, satisfying the growing demand which was created by the new flying shuttles which had hugely increased the quantity of yarn which could be woven into cloth. Farmers and workers in the cottage industries such as spinning and weaving became the new urban proletariat which carried the economic success of the country, but hardly profited from it.

On the continent, the French Revolution stirred up social

and political unrest in other countries, too. England found itself siding with the main continental powers such as Prussia, Russia and the Habsburg Empire and played a major role in the Napoleonic wars: the battle of Trafalgar not only shot Admiral Nelson into the stratosphere of eternal heroes, but it gave the allied troops control of the sea; and you know of course that the Duke of Wellington, together with Prussian troops, put paid to the Corsican's ambitions.

I already mentioned the 'Peterloo Massacre' – these protests were only one of many incidents marking a period of unrest. The ideas of the enlightenment and of the French Revolution had found their way to England; the writings of Thomas Paine, who promoted the equality of men, were the bestselling books in the late eighteenth and early nineteenth centuries. England, through its early and swift industrialisation, faced the same problem as other large nations in Europe: the dynamism of the lower and middle classes was obstructed by an unphased upper class which had no feeling for and no interest in the everyday lives of the massive majority of the people.

Civil unrest found an early culmination in the 'Luddite' movement – a name which is used today to disqualify anyone who dares to object to unbridled economic growth and technological change. Yes, the original Luddites did their bit of machine-storming, but they had every reason to do so. I have already mentioned the introduction of flying spools and Spinning Jennies in the textile industry, which made poorly paid pieceworkers out of highly skilled labourers. It is unlikely that a person called 'Ned Ludd' or 'King Ludd' ever existed, but his name served as cover for those who wrote political pamphlets about the plight of the workers and, seeing that these protests were greeted with utter disdain by the Powers That Be, embarked on more decisive action. They had every reason to look for such a cover: ever since the early nineteenth century, destruction of machinery had been punishable by death. From about 1811, the movement spread from Nottingham throughout Yorkshire and Lancashire, where Manchester had evolved into the world's biggest centre for the textile industry. Workers destroyed machines and whole factories; the owners of these industrial hell-holes were threatened and at least one of these early captains of industry was killed.

The authorities reacted forcefully; the military was ordered into the areas of unrest, and at times, there were more English soldiers occupied in beating down the Luddites than fighting Napoleon. Two mighty clashes between protesters and the military occurred, and finally, in 1813, the ringleaders were rounded up and brought to court. The judges did not go easy in those days: seventeen Luddite leaders were executed, the others deported.

These judgments may have brought an end to the Luddite movement, but it did not solve the problem. The movement had been a desperate cry for help by people who saw their lives reduced to ruins. It was too early for them to be heard – real social reforms took another 50 years to arrive.

Where the Luddites had challenged the authorities with their violent actions, another group of men who called attention to their desperate situation were made to suffer despite their almost Gandhiesque, non-violent conduct: the Tolpuddle Martyrs. This was a group of six men from the eponymous village in Dorset who had formed a 'friendly society' in 1832. Their aim: getting a wage that would allow them to survive.

Next to the textile industry, agriculture was going through the toughest structural changes. As the expensive new machines needed to be operated on large stretches of land, the authorities permitted large-scale 'enclosures' of communal land which had previously been used by smallholding farmers, who were turned into paid labourers, either in the cities or in the agricultural industry. Higher productivity meant lower prices for food, which in turn lead to lower wages for farm workers. The men from Tolpuddle demanded nothing more than the living wage of ten shillings per week, which was accepted as the absolute minimum at the time. Their real wages had just fallen to seven shillings per week, and the landowners had already announced a further cut to six shillings.

The Tolpuddle men did not destroy property or take up arms – they wrote pamphlets and petitioned their Members of Parliament. These could not care less, and the authorities used an obscure law that prohibited people from forming societies and sealing their union with an oath. This was what our friends had done; they were arrested, tried and deported for seven years. The obvious injustice caused a huge public outcry: 800,000 people signed petitions to parliament, and the men were pardoned and returned to England.

The actions of the Tolpuddle Martyrs are perceived as the start of the trade union movement in England; every year, there is a festival to honour the brave men. Four of them could not bear staying in England upon their return from deportation and emigrated to Canada. You can visit their graves in London. London, Ontario, that is.

Over time, some things did change: slavery was abolished in 1807 (slave traders received £20 million in compensation) and formally outlawed in 1833. The voting system was reformed; prior to this, cities such as Manchester or Leeds did not have a Member of Parliament. Child labour was regulated: working children had to be at least nine years old and they had to be at least thirteen years of age before they could legally work more than eight hours per day.

To understand England's economic status at the time, one needs to look at a couple of figures: half of the world's production of steel, coal and textiles came from the Kingdom. Transport had been revolutionised by a system of canals which measured some 4,000 miles. In 1825, the world's first steam train ran between the north-western towns of Stockton and Darlington; in 1830 the first passenger train ran between Liverpool and Manchester (killing its most ardent political supporter in a freak accident during the maiden voyage). In 1863, the London Underground started operating, the first such system in the world.

England was a proud industrial nation, and when the old enemy across the Channel staged an industrial show in Paris in 1844, national pride demanded that the world be reminded of England's achievements: enter the 'Great Exhibition', which was held in Hyde Park in 1851, organised by Prince Albert. The building was a marvel: the purpose-built 'Crystal Palace' was some 500 metres long and 150 metres wide. It was erected in a record nine months, and after the exhibition, it was re-assembled in south west London. The giant conservatory burnt down in 1936 – how an edifice made entirely of steel and glass can burn down is beyond me.

England was a seriously rich nation, but despite its economic prowess, it did not lift a finger when disaster struck in its oldest colony: Ireland. In 1845, the troublesome island was struck by potato blight; over the next seven years, more than a million people died of starvation, another million left the country. When the Irish cried for help, the English shrugged their shoulders, said something about the invisible hand of the markets and went to have lunch.

England became thoroughly urbanised in the nineteenth century; around 1850, more than half of the population lived in towns and cities. Within 100 years, the number of inhabitants had tripled to 21 million even though the living conditions in the sprawling cities had been efficient in keeping the life expectancy low. It was Friedrich Engels who described the living conditions of the urban poor in graphic detail. His *The Condition of the Working Classes in England in 1844* in which he calls the treatment of the urban poor 'social murder', makes gruesome reading. Even if one is an ardent opponent of Marx's and Engels's analysis of society, one cannot help but be moved by descriptions such as the one given by a priest who said about his parish in the East London borough of Bethnal Green:

It contains 1,400 houses, inhabited by 2,795 families, or about 12,000 persons. The space upon which this large population dwells, is less than 400 yards (1,200 feet) square, and in this overcrowding it is nothing unusual to find a man, his wife, four or five children, and, sometimes, both grandparents, all in one single room, where they eat, sleep, and work. I believe that before the Bishop of London called attention to this most poverty-stricken parish, people at the West End knew as little of it as of the savages of Australia or the South Sea Isles. And if we make ourselves acquainted with these unfortunates, through personal observation, if we watch them at their scanty meal and see them bowed by illness and want of work, we shall find such a mass of helplessness and misery, that a nation like ours must blush that these things can be possible. I was rector near Huddersfield during the three years in which the mills were at their worst, but I have never seen such complete helplessness of the poor as since then in Bethnal Green. Not one father of a family in ten in the whole neighbourhood has other clothing than his working suit, and that is as bad and tattered as possible; many, indeed, have no other covering for the night than these rags, and no bed, save a sack of straw and shavings.

There were no proper sanitation, waste disposal or sewage systems in the boom towns and cities such as Manchester or Leeds; in London, where there had been efforts at cleaning up the city since the Middle Ages, the infrastructure simply could not cope. We may read Charles Dickens's novels today as delightful rags-to-riches stories: but the squalor, the brutality and the heartlessness that characters such as Oliver Twist had to endure were hardly fictitious. The Victorian work ethic was cruel; if you were poor, now that was just too bad. Perhaps you should have tried more? Yes, charity was regarded as a virtue, and giving to the poor was encouraged. But one did not want them to get lazy.

In 1840, almost 60 per cent of Manchester's working class children died before the age of five. To alleviate the problem, some industrialists constructed model settlements for their workers. Of course, these projects were hailed as symbols of a reformed, benign capitalism. As nice as these new settlements were, benevolence was not always the driving force behind them; weak and ailing workers are not very productive. So the 'benevolence' was often more a kind of 'enlightened self-interest' that brought handsome profits in terms of maintaining a trained workforce and keeping up productivity. And until the middle of the nineteenth century, many employers expanded their profits by paying their workers in scrip, which meant that they could only buy the provisions they needed from shops run by the very companies which employed them.

Buckingham Palace, London

*Where we will meet an Empress
and become very well behaved indeed*

William IV, the jolly sailor, tried not to get involved too deeply in the tedious business of government but he had a superb sense of timing. He duly closed his eyes in 1837, a month after his niece Victoria had celebrated her eighteenth birthday and had thus become fully qualified to get to the throne.

She was also the first monarch to occupy Buckingham Palace as her official London residence. George III had bought the house in 1761 as a private residence, and it had been extended and altered over the next 75 years. 'Buck House', as the palace is often called, is certainly not a beautiful building; the design resembles an assortment of boxes which have been welded together. But it seems to do just fine for the royal families who have lived here over the past 175 years. And its balcony is so convenient for waving to the adoring crowds, isn't it?

When Victoria moved in, nobody would have thought that this young woman would set the record for the longest-serving monarch in English history. She spent 63 years and seven months on the throne – Elizabeth II will have to soldier on until 2016 to equal this achievement. We keep our fingers crossed and wish Her Majesty good health. Sorry, Charles. Victoria was the first and only Empress on the English throne, thanks to her reign over India.

During her years, England came to rule a quarter of the world but it was not good enough for Hanover: the little kingdom in northern Germany did not accept a female monarch, so the union of the two very unequal states was terminated, after 130 years.

Victoria abstained from day-to-day politics, a wise move if ever there was one. She accepted her largely ceremonial role and did what was expected of her: first she selected a trusty companion, her cousin Prince Albert Saxe-Coburg-Gotha, to further limit the royal gene pool; then she went forth and multiplied. She produced nine children, who were dispatched all over the continent to prop up the European royal families. When the troops met in battle during the First World War, most of them served the royal brothers, sisters and cousins of their enemies' kings.

When Victoria married, she wore a white wedding dress, setting a precedent and creating a tradition that has gripped women all over the world ever since. Her marriage may have been the exception to the rule that royal marriages are purely functional arrangements. The Queen and her husband set a public example of marital harmony, which came as a welcome change from the days of George IV and his successor, William IV. They even seem to have been genuinely devoted to each other; when Albert died prematurely in 1861, the Queen put on her black mourning dress, never again to be seen wearing another colour. Her compatriots, however, don't seem to have been too fond of her – there were at least five attempts to kill her and she was wounded in one of them.

Victoria's black dresses symbolised a sea-change in English public life that occurred during her reign. England, which had for most of its history enjoyed a reputation as a land of revelry and exceptionally good food, developed into a drab and dreary land of rigid morality, bigotry and a general cult of not enjoying oneself. At least that was the impression the ruling classes were eager to make.

Sex became a no-no in polite society, even though Victoria never indicated that she shunned the pleasures of the body. She enjoyed drawing naked men, and her nine children are evidence of a healthy appetite for marital rompey-pompey. Still, times change and any show of emotion in public was seriously frowned upon. One just did not mention the names of any parts of the body, especially those located 'south of the equator'. Until 1861, homosexuality, 'the love that dare not speak its name', was punishable by death. It remained a crime for many years afterward, and several notable figures, including Oscar Wilde, were imprisoned.

Of course, this 'holier than thou'-attitude reeked of hypocrisy and cynicism. Giving to the poor helped placate the conscience of the givers and ameliorated some of the most visible symptoms of deprivation. But this doctoring did not cure the social disease that plagued the country. Living and working conditions remained utterly desperate, and the official rigidity of public morals contrasted heavily with the saucy private enjoyments; at no time were there as many prostitutes in England; vaudeville theatre thrived, as did pornographic writings; child labour remained legal and there was vociferous advocacy for not extending too much education to the poor, so as not to arouse their aspirations.

Victoria's reign is often perceived as peaceful – which of course it wasn't. Colonial wars and scuffles abounded, but much of it went unnoticed because the battles were not fought in Europe. Not all of these campaigns were successful: when English troops invaded Afghanistan in 1839, just one member of the 16,000-strong expeditionary force returned to India. When the weak Chinese government tried to block the import of opium, the English conducted a quick and savage 'Opium War' to guard this lucrative business. During the Crimean War, the incompetence of the British command sent 600 young cavalry men to face the Russian canons – 'into the valley of death they rode' as Alfred Tennyson writes in his commemorative poem. Some 80 years later, Winston Churchill halted the Yalta conference to pay the site of this disastrous attack a visit. And the great English leader during the Second World War also played a role in the last big war during Victoria's reign: he reported on the Boer War and did not mince his words when condemning the English invention of concentration camps for non-combatant Boers, which led to the deaths of thousands of women and children.

Victoria, the saintly, moral, mourning widow on the throne; Victoria, the war criminal and drug overlord whose troops savagely oppressed any opposition to colonial rule – there are two very distinct sides to this coin. She died in 1901, in the presence of her grandson, Kaiser Wilhelm II. Edward VII took over, the first English king to bear the Saxe-Coburg Gotha name. The family rebranded itself 'Windsor' in 1917 – it was no longer cool, even for royals, to have a German name.

Liverpool, Merseyside

*Where we ponder the Empire and
those who had it happen to them*

We all know Liverpool as the home of The Beatles and of two football clubs, one of them (Liverpool FC) great, and the other (Everton FC) a great failure, at least in most years. Liverpool is home to the most deprived boroughs in the country. With more than 30 unemployed workers for every open position, the city's council announced in 2011 that the unemployment rate had reached 41 per cent.

But Liverpool is also home to the oldest professional symphonic orchestra in England and a treasure-trove of splendid architecture. These riches have a dark source: the triangular trade, which was one of the most cynical business inventions in world history. The splendid Maritime Museum in Liverpool gives a heart-wrenching account of the atrocities that came with this trade; we will come to that later.

Let's talk about the Empire. I would never say that the English are 'xenophobic', because it would not be very nice to do so. Let's perhaps agree that they have an actively neutral position when it comes to foreigners. Many English will tell you that some of their best friends know people who know foreigners.

This attitude is, of course, rooted in history. A proud nation that once ruled a quarter of the globe cannot be blamed for thinking of itself as being a cut above the rest of us. Where other nations indulged in robbery, piracy and slave trading, these expressions could not possibly be used in polite English society. The millions of people who died as a direct result of England's colonial expansion were mere collateral damage – after all, what's a little bit of hanging and flogging and maiming when you have exported cricket and imported curry houses? And even though England may have lost most of her colonies, the global reign of English as a *lingua franca* provides a very stable source of income for the publishing, music and film industries, business schools, language teachers and other ventures.

England's expansion beyond its wet frontiers started in the twelfth century, when Ireland was usurped. When Spanish, Italian and Portuguese sailors started scouring the globe for new lands, England lagged behind by a couple of decades. The first formal colony was set up in North America at the end of the sixteenth century; the Caribbean with Barbados, the Bahamas, Jamaica and a slew of other islands followed soon after. England set up trading posts and footholds in Africa, which were needed to support the triangular trade. In the eighteenth century, India and Canada were added to the portfolio and Captain Cook saw to it that the Union Jack flew over Australia and large parts of Oceania, as well. Despite losing America, this made for a pretty impressive array of possessions, and cartographers indulged in colouring the world in pink.

Colonialism was not motivated by the quest for holiday homes in benevolent climates. Greed, simple and raw, was the foundation of the whole exercise. The English never really came up with other explanations; yes, missionaries were sent out to save the troubled souls of the natives, but one didn't endeavour to climb the giddy heights of PR that the French reached with their *mission civilisatrice*. Gold and silver, precious stones and spices, and especially sugar, cotton and tobacco came to England, where they were processed and sold on, creating huge riches for everyone involved. London, Bristol and Liverpool were the centres of the trade and the cities prospered thanks to the human misery their worthy citizens caused to millions of people.

In the triangular trade, which started in the 1660s, slavery was the cornerstone of the economic success. It went thus: English traders loaded their ships with goods such as cloth, tools and appliances, beer, brandy and so forth and dispatched them to 'Guinea', which meant anywhere in West Africa. Along the coast, the European colonial powers had established a network of ports and fortifications which served the hinterland; for the English, the 'Royal Africa Company' organised the business. The hinterland served the ports by buying many of the goods imported from England and by delivering slaves, which were hunted by indigenous warrior chiefs. The wretched victims of these hunts were sold on to the European traders, who first branded them with irons and then put them on their ships bound for the Americas.

The conditions on the slave ships during this 'Middle Passage' were atrocious; the people were shackled and stacked like sardines in the cargo holds, forced to lie in excrement and urine, being able to escape their foul conditions only once or twice a day to be given a breath of fresh air, some water and a little soup. Other ships avoided slave ships for the noxious stink emanating from them; almost 20 per cent of the human cargo aboard these ships never survived the trip. It was not unheard of for the captains of these ships to throw some of the slaves overboard to combat diseases and, of course, to be able to cash in on the insurance. Especially towards the end of the slave trade, when the French and English navies actively pursued the remaining slave transports, many slaves were drowned to avoid run-ins with the law.

Once the slave ships landed in the Americas, the survivors of the 'Middle Passage' were sold on to local slave merchants, who in turn supplied them to the thriving cotton and sugar plantations in the Caribbean and the southern regions of what became the USA. After a thorough clean-up, the ships were loaded with new cargo – the precious raw materials I mentioned earlier. Back in England, the ships loaded products generated from these materials for sale in Africa, as part of the price one had to pay for the slaves, and the journey started anew.

The trips lasted up to eighteen months, and the Liverpool traders alone organised on average more than 100 triangular journeys per year. The gruesome business yielded extremely high returns, and by the time slavery was abolished in 1807, some 3.5 million people had been trafficked by the English alone – a third of all slaves brought to the Americas.

In India, the English had their own ways of securing lasting friendships: those Indians who did not see that having an Empress in London was part of the natural order of things, tended to find themselves tied to the muzzle of a canon and blown to smithereens. A peaceful protest in Amritsar in 1919 ended with the protesters confined to a small park, surrounded by high walls. The heroic English soldiers mounted machine guns on these walls and mowed down the fearsome enemy. In Australia, English benevolence reduced the aboriginal population from almost 700,000 to 90,000 in under a century.

Where the restless natives had effective weapons and tactics at hand, the going was tougher for the English: the American colonists are perhaps the most famous example of such resistance, and I already mentioned the Afghan disaster and the concentration camps installed during the Boer War. The Zulus also gave the English troops in South Africa a bitter run for their money, as did the zealots of Muhammad Ahmad, the self-declared 'Mahdi' (saviour) during the eponymous uprising in Sudan in 1883.

The Sudanese wrested control of the capital city Khartoum from the English, killing the hapless General Charles Gordon in the process. Gordon had been called out of retirement and dispatched to Africa under the mistaken assumption that he would easily wipe the floor with the natives. Being outnumbered by the Mahdi forces, he went into English colonial mode: wave the flag, ignore the facts and make a gallant last stand. Instead of leading his troops out of Khartoum, he held out. His troops were butchered; the general, whose headless strategy had triggered the disaster, found himself beheaded. You can still see Gordon's statue on the bank of the Nile. A glorious hero, indeed.

The Empire lasted until the mid-twentieth century. The big 'white' settler colonies such as Canada, Australia, New Zealand and South Africa had gained their independence some decades before, but the real end came with the independence of India in 1947. Africa followed in the 1950s and 1960s. The Falklands War in 1982 and the return of Hong Kong to Chinese rule in 1997 were perhaps the most poignant reminders of the colonial era in recent times. Today, fourteen territories still form part of Britain; from the Virgin Islands to Gibraltar, an astonishing number of them are havens for tax dodgers. Even the buildings rented by Her Majesty's Revenue and Customs department are run from one of these tax oases. Which brings modern day buccaneering back to its origins: whether you set out to capture Spanish galleons in the old days or you just wish to trick Her Majesty out of taxes today, the former colonies provide the perfect place to start.

Brick Lane, East London

Where we have a curry and look at colours

O ne tangible result of former colonial grandeur is the strong presence of non-white people in the major English cities. Although people of African, South Asian or Chinese origin had been living in England for more than 500 years, the big wave of immigration came after the Second World War. The arrival of the *Empire Windrush* from the Caribbean marks the beginning of England's slow transformation into a multicultural society. After the independence and partition of the South Asian empire (India, Pakistan, Sri Lanka), immigration from this area exploded, followed by another wave of South Asian immigrants after their expulsion from Uganda in the 1970s.

Brick Lane in London's East End is one area which on some days may look out of place with its huge South Asian population, and its shops and restaurants catering for them. But it is not the only place in England where you can find such strong concentrations of immigrants.

In a recent interview, the Tory MP Kwasi Kwarteng (who has Ghanaian heritage) remarked that the only way to understand the way the country has developed over the last few years was to understand the impact of the empire. I tend to agree: without the imperial past, there would be no multicultural present.

If you want to get a sense of the immigrant experience, you could do worse than picking up books by authors such as C.L.R. James or Sam Selvon, who have recorded the early years; younger writers such as Zadie Smith or Monica Ali portray the present situation, which – despite the official policy of multiculturalism – is marked by deep divisions between the various ethnic groups who make up England's population today.

Two of England's most popular TV presenters, Trevor MacDonald and Moira Stewart, are of Caribbean origin. They may have been the nation's darlings since the 1970s, but this should not distort our perception of society, just as the great number of dark-skinned footballers, or the many cricketers of Caribbean and South Asian heritage in the respective English national teams does not mean that England does not remain largely segregated along racial boundaries.

Millions of people come to England every year, on holiday, on business, and many come here with the hope of finding a better place to live, a place to carve out a future. England has an allure that speaks to the masses, and it has done so throughout its existence, even before there was any such thing as 'England'. The history of the British Isles is a history of continuous immigration. The hunter-gatherers who followed their prey and ended up in the Peak District were at the beginning of this immigration; the bankers from Frankfurt or Paris or Shanghai settling in the City of London today, hunting for profits and bonuses, may look a tad different, and they may wield different weapons, but in the end they are not much more than strategically-shaved versions of their forebears, which is especially visible on Friday evenings in most pubs in the City.

The English struggle with the concept of the foreigner even when they venture abroad themselves. If strangers dare to come to the Sceptred Isle, a general displeasure can hardly be concealed. Mind you, we have come a long way since 1968 when the Tory MP Enoch Powell gave a speech in which he warned that continued immigration would lead to massive problems, alluding to Virgil's *Aeneid* and the 'River Tiber foaming with much blood'. Nobody with half a wit and sense of propriety would repeat such words today and even the most conservative Tories will tell you that they embrace today's multicultural society whole-heartedly.

England, and especially London, is probably the most cosmopolitan place in Europe. Around the turn of the century, London's people spoke 307 languages – no other city in the world can boast such a variety. English leads the way, with Bengali (which is native to the south-west of India and Bangladesh) in second place; there are more than 100 African languages spoken in London.

Impressive as this may be, the integration of immigrant communities has not worked too well. There is still hardly any inter-marriage between the European, Asian, African or

Middle Eastern communities. In most large towns and cities, you will find ethnically defined areas, most of which sprung up thanks to the administrative belief that these homogenous communities can be managed much easier than heterogeneous ones. Add to this the Thatcherite principle of selling off council housing stock to more affluent tenants, thus pushing the economically challenged into the direst settlements, and you end up with a combination of institutional racism and class distinctions – the perfect recipe for ethnic tensions. Ethnic tensions do flare up from time to time, such as the riots in Oldham, Burnley and other northern cities, where the right-wing BNP has achieved electoral success with up to 16 per cent of the votes in past years. Some years ago, the Tory minister Norman Tebbitt claimed that many immigrants were failing the 'cricket test': as long as your heart is with the English team, you can consider yourself at home. Very helpful, don't you think?

Yes, there are many non-European faces on English television, and you will see a number of non-white Members of Parliament and in leading positions in industry. But these are exceptions. Young black males are subject to stop-searching (which is legal only if there is a specific suspicion of a crime being carried out) ten times more often than their white compatriots; even black celebrities, such as John Sentamu, the Archbishop of York, and Formula 1 champion Lewis Hamilton, have been subjected to this practice.

The recent riots of 2011, when parts of London were laid

to waste, may have borne some of the hallmarks of racial conflicts, but these excesses were fuelled not by racial, but social segregation; these two evils tend to co-exist in unsavoury conjunction. One in three youths living in the capital say they own no books; 20 per cent of school leavers cannot read or write properly. Without a solution to these problems, multiculturalism will remain an act of window dressing.

Heathrow, London

*Where we stand in line with many others
and have some time to think about the English
and everybody else*

Where do you come from? Or rather: Where were you, before you came here? Moscow? New York? Ouagadougou? It does not matter. Leave it behind. You are in England now.

If you happen to have arrived at Heathrow, Europe's busiest airport, you will have been given a first taste of what a truly English welcome can be like. Hundreds of people are queuing up, letting themselves be processed by security controls and immigration. It does not matter whether you are Scandinavian or Asian, Dutch or African: you are an 'Alien' now. Think of E.T. – you may not look like him but to the English there is not much of a difference. Try as you might, there will always be an England and you may be allowed to visit, but becoming part of it is another matter entirely.

'What's an Englishman with an inferiority complex?' asked comedian Paul Merton, and his answer: 'He thinks he's as good as anybody else.' It's a nice joke in the best tradition of self-deprecating English humour, but our English friends have a very clear idea when it comes to their status in the world. As the arch-imperialist Cecil Rhodes puts it, 'Remember that you are an Englishman, and have consequently won first prize in the lottery of life.'

These soundbites may be taken in good humour by those of us who have to eke out our miserable existence beyond the reaches of Her Majesty's benevolent reign – but sometimes, the jest expresses truth. To put it plainly: the English are not particularly fond of foreigners, and they divide them roughly into four categories: the Celtic neighbours, French and Germans, the Lost Cousins in America; everyone else.

The English and their Celtic neighbours from Wales, Scotland and Ireland have led an uneasy cohabitation in the British Isles for centuries, almost always with the understanding that the English are the ones who are calling the shots. For us foreigners, it is quite normal to call the whole set-up simply 'England', much to the chagrin of ardent nationalists who try to protect the perceived identities of the Celts, at times with a fury that hints at a massive inferiority complex.

And the English are well aware of these complexes, and they are not shy about expressing their resentment for their Celtic neighbours. This may have to do with the fact that there are no written mementos of Celtic history; their culture was oral, their memories are buried with the druids and chiefs. Even festivals such as the Eisteddfod, which gets together manly choirs from all over Wales, are recent inventions; the Eisteddfod was created in 1792, born out of the romantic interest in all things reminiscent of the Dark Ages.

The English have firm ideas about their neighbours. Their reaction to former prime minister, Gordon Brown, was a classic example of what the English think about the Scots. We have already heard P.G. Wodehouse's verdict 'It is never difficult to distinguish between a Scotsman with a grievance and a ray of sunshine.' Scots are 'dour', meaning they are not very funny or cheerful. But they are generally trustworthy, which is why call centres are setting up shop north of Hadrian's Wall, employing Caledonia's children to flog double glazing, insurance or electric blankets.

The Welsh take on the role of goblins in the English imagination. They run around in green valleys and have dubious relations with sheep; they spend their lives in coal pits; they tend to sing at the slightest provocation and they are all called Evans or Rhys or Jones. You may remember that I told you about TV presenter Anne Robinson asking 'What are the Welsh for?' – and nobody being able to give a proper answer.

The Irish are right at the bottom of the pile; the English either despise them or think they're a bit of a joke. One can have a very good time with the Irish; on weekends, you will find Dublin heaving with English revellers, but rarely are the 'Paddies' taken seriously. England's first colony has always been the rebellious poorhouse; most Irish are Catholic, which is still a bit of a no-no in England, and they made up most of the *lumpenproletariat* in England's industrial centres. In 1729, the great satirist Jonathan Swift, himself Irish, commented on the desperate plight of his countrymen in his *A Modest Proposal for Preventing the Children of Poor People From Being a Burden on Their Parents or Country, and for Making Them Beneficial to the Publick*, suggesting that the Irish have an ample supply of children, which may well be used for feeding the rich in England:

> I grant this food may be somewhat dear, and therefore very proper for Landlords, who as they have already devoured most of the Parents, seem to have the best Title to the Children. [...] For this kind of commodity will not bear exportation, and flesh being of too tender a consistence, to admit a long continuance in salt, although perhaps I could name a country, which would be glad to eat up our whole nation without it.

The Irish image was not really improved by the separatist uprising in Northern Ireland, which saw terrorist attacks being perpetrated not only on Irish soil but in England's city centres as well. The 1974 Prevention of Terrorism Act held more or less all Irish responsible for all terrorist atrocities. The act led to spectacular miscarriages of justice, putting many innocent people behind bars for years.

The deep sympathy the English hold for their neighbours is aptly reflected in some ancient bylaws in some towns and cities: In Chester, you may shoot at Welsh people with a bow and arrow after midnight and within the city's walls;

in Hereford you may express yourself with more ease, given that the Welsh are only protected on Sundays and within the grounds of the cathedral; in York, you can pick up your bow and arrow and hunt Scots at all times, except Sundays.

The French and the Germans are the old, eternal enemies, and possibly the only European nations that the English would grudgingly regard as almost up to their own level. Which means that the old and trusted weapon, humour, is rigorously employed to deal with both nations; 'frogs' and 'krauts' are just two loving monikers applied to these people. (The French call the English 'les rosbifs', so the food motive seems to work on both sides of the Channel.)

The Frenchmen are 'frogs' because they obviously indulge in frogs' legs at all times. And of course they eat smelly cheeses, quaff champagne, conduct numerous love affairs, are interested in all sorts of philosophies, hang out in cafés, speak English with a horrible accent and murder pop music. More than that: the French occupy a country which the English seem to think should by rights belong to them – there is that Noman heritage, after all! Well, the French won't be easily shifted to other parts of the world, which leaves only one course of action: buy it. No other nation has been as acquisitive when it comes to dilapidated properties and today, there are wide stretches in Brittany, Normandy and the Dordogne where you will be able to spend a fortnight's holiday without speaking a word of French.

The Germans are either 'krauts' or 'huns'; the first

nickname continues the food theme in the naming of nations in an enchanting way. Krauts became the pejorative term for Germans in the First World War, but it really isn't that pejorative. At least that is what the Advertising Standards Agency decreed some years ago when the German embassy complained about the use of the word in advertising. Germans are not vegetables, the embassy argued. No sense of humour, obviously!

While Franco-English relations have been bad for centuries, owing to the turf wars on both sides of the Channel that had started almost immediately after the Normans had invaded England, German-English relations have been quite cordial most of the time. The countries were allies in many wars on the continent; German troops were deployed to combat the rebellious Americans during the War of Independence, and England and Prussia also joined forces to put an end to that pan-European troublemaker, Napoleon Bonaparte, at the Battle of Waterloo. The fact that English monarchs have hailed from German ancestry for the past 300 years did help for most of the time, and even the kingdom's anthem is German in origin – by singing 'God Save the Queen', the English inadvertently pay tribute to their Teutonic relatives, and even the 'Sterling' is an homage to Germanic values: the term came into use to depict the high quality of coins minted in Germany.

The two World Wars, however, have soured the relationship and whenever some crisis unfolds involving both nations

– such as the English football team having to face the mighty enemy, or Germany and France getting their way in European politics – references to the Nazi era come up quick and loud. 'Only Jews and Arabs are hated more than the Germans', wrote the *Guardian*. Jeremy Clarkson, the non-thinking man's car show presenter, greeted the new Mini by giving a Nazi salute; the wonderful comedy series *Fawlty Towers* will forever be remembered for the scene in which John Cleese goose-steps around the hotel, telling the complaining German guests that they have no sense of humour. He may have been conked over the head prior to this, but don't we all know that the concussed and drunk speak the truth?

Oh well. As a German, I have learnt over the years not to be offended. I am an optimist. In such moments I tell myself that there must be at least one brain cell somewhere in the kingdom. And maybe, someday, someone will find it.

As for the Lost Cousins, 'England and America are two countries separated by a common language', said George Bernard Shaw (and Oscar Wilde, Winston Churchill and many others have said similar things) and he is, of course, right. When it comes to the lost cousins across the sea, the English are torn between abject scorn for the nation that wears down everything that may be called civilisation, and delirious admiration for the powerful nation populated by one's own sons and daughters – the USA may have been independent for a while, but, let's be honest, they are our kith and kin, don't you know.

You may find many advocates of the latter attitude among the loony fringes of the Eurosceptic parties; some of them will also argue that the continental drift which, centimetre by centimetre, cuts the distance between the British Isles and America, is reason enough to quit the European Union and join the North American Free Trade Agreement.

Much of the positive attitude towards the USA is owed to the assistance the cousins gave during the two World Wars. Without this support, the kingdom would not have been able to withstand the Nazi onslaught, bearing in mind that it had been cut off from the continent and thus from its vital food imports. The Americans proved themselves to be trustworthy friends in the darkest hour.

This, of course, does not mean that any English comedian worth his salt would dream of not calling Americans lazy, fat and stupid.

The rest of the world is not of too much importance to the English, apart from the 'white' Commonwealth, meaning Canada, Australia, South Africa and New Zealand, and of course the lost 'jewel in the crown', India. All other countries merely exist in their function of providing dry spots in the oceans and destinations for English youngsters on their Gap Year between school and college, offering labour, sex and sun-burn. Some countries, especially former colonies in South Asia and Africa, are quite useful for providing well-educated doctors, nurses and teachers who fill the gaps created by spending cuts to the English education system. And since the Iron Curtain came down, well-trained plumbers, builders and handymen from Central and Eastern Europe have created stiff competition for the old hordes of English cowboy tradesmen. Previously, when you called a plumber, you could be sure that he would turn up three weeks late, convert your basement into an indoor pool and vanish without a trace. That may still happen, but at least it will be considerably cheaper!

Lancing, West Sussex

A place where many people speak some languages but monoglotism rules

My first trip to England brought me to the seaside town of Lancing, and therefore we have come here to take a look at language. Lancing boasts a minor public school, which was attended by one of my favourite writers, Evelyn Waugh (despite the name, he was a man). Apart from this, Lancing does not have much to boast about. We might have chosen other destinations, but this is as good as any.

The French have their *Académie française* to guard the purity of the nation's language, the South Africans have the 'Taal Monument' in Paarl as a tribute to Afrikaans. The English have – their language. But do they really? No language in the history of the world has had such reach. And I would venture that, given the fact that English has become the only globally understood language, it has been wrested out of the control of its traditional owners. Who is to say that the English used by a Chinese and a Mexican to communicate about business is wrong? If it works for them, fine!

Fortunately, the English tend to be rather pragmatic about it. Why should one go into a sulk if someone gets the odd preposition wrong, or if a foreigner falls into one of the many traps set up when it comes to pronunciation? Yes, one tends to giggle if an American pronounces 'Worcestershire' as it is spelt, or if a German or Frenchman cannot get his tongue around the 'th'-sound, but what really matters is that they all speak English, or at least try to speak it. And this sets all these foreigners apart from the true Englishman.

A proper Englishman doesn't speak foreign languages. Why should he? If more than a billion people around the globe have learned English or are in the process of doing so, and five billion others have the opportunity to do so, why should the fifty million English bother to learn any of these other languages? After all, it does work for everyone involved.

Honestly, I cannot really find a pragmatic argument that would put this monoglotist position in its place. And the English education system has not come up with one either. Yes, pupils have to learn a foreign language from an early age for a couple of years (89 per cent choose French), but they do not have to take an exam in it. Contrast that with my own experience: in my day, you could not enter a German university without English and at least one other foreign language. Around the turn of the century, the French and German ambassadors in London embarked upon a campaign to promote foreign languages in schools. To their exasperation they were rebuffed by the education ministry, which argued that more investment in foreign languages may not provide the best value for money.

Most of my English friends find such attitudes embarrassing. But maybe these attitudes have their foundation in that other English trait, the fear of standing out? If you can master a foreign language and demonstrate your proficiency, it might be regarded as showing off; and this would not be acceptable. Which is why Aunt Judy will face her family's taunts when she utters a properly-pronounced '*Merci bien*' when shopping for cheap booze across the channel. 'Ooh, she's quite the linguist, isn't she?'

We foreigners may sometimes despair at this specific quirk of our English neighbours. But we all love their pop music, their TV series and their literature – 70 per cent of all books translated worldwide are translated from the English. 'So,' my non-German-speaking English friend may say, 'what's the problem?' And that would be it.

Oxbridge, Knowledgeshire

*Where we could have learnt many things,
had we been admitted*

Runs it not here, the track by Childsworth Farm,
Past the high wood, to where the elm-tree crowns
The hill behind whose ridge the sunset flames?
The signal-elm, that looks on Ilsley Downs,
The Vale, the three lone wears, the youthful Thames? —
This winter-eve is warm,
Humid the air! leafless, yet soft as spring,
The tender purple spray on copse and briers!
And that sweet city with her dreaming spires,
She needs not June for beauty's heightening,

Matthew Arnold, *Thyrsis*, 1865

Dear reader, as you can gather from the title of this chapter, we are travelling to a place that does not exist. Or rather to two places which do exist, but whose reputation has transcended their location. Oxford and Cambridge, two cities at a distance of around 150 kilometres from each other, are among the strongest pillars of England's reputation in the world. Two seats of learning, both of them ancient, who continue to be seen as world leaders in science and humanities, in research and teaching. When it comes to prestige, they are only rivalled by the top Ivy League universities in the USA. If you are lucky enough to be accepted at one of the colleges which make up these universities, your future looks bright. People simply assume that a graduate of Oxford or Cambridge is special; and there is no one to discourage this thinking.

Even we foreigners know that there is fierce competition between the two universities; the annual Boat Race is watched by millions both at home and abroad, it is also one of the most important events in England's social calendar. The universities compete in almost any sport you can imagine, and wearing the dark blue of Oxford and the light blue of Cambridge on the sporting field is one of the highest honours that can be bestowed on a student.

Looking at the cities that come with these universities, you will find that they are both dominated by the architecture of the colleges, some of which date back to the Middle Ages. Matthew Arnold's famous poem about Oxford, which I quote at the beginning of this chapter, refers to this feature. Oxford has always had a strong merchant and industrial background; being close to where the kings and noblemen roamed, it has been privileged with the attention of the Powers That Be for centuries. Cambridge has also always been a prosperous market town; but where Oxford conveys the atmosphere of a dynamic and busy place of business, Cambridge maintains an aura of peacefulness. This difference is hardly a matter of size: Oxford has about 160,000 inhabitants, Cambridge around 120,000. Perhaps this difference is owed to the 'Backs' in Cambridge; the huge park-like areas, which stretch from the River Cam to the back side of the colleges and make one feel as if one is a visitor to a majestic garden city.

Oxford became a seat of learning quite early; legend has it that King Alfred came here in the late ninth century to rest and that he discovered the citizens to be exceptionally learned. The founding date of the university is not known; it is assumed that it started operations in the late eleventh century, which puts it on par with the universities of Bologna and Paris as one of the oldest universities in Europe. It was from Paris that the major impulse for the growth of Oxford came, when all foreigners were expelled from there in 1167.

Bearing in mind that Oxford had been a thriving trading centre for a long time before the university was established, quarrels between the scholarly community and the local Oxford citizens were frequent. It is assumed that a particularly severe confrontation between 'town and gown' led a group of scholars to decamp further east, to Cambridge, where that university was founded in 1209. Both universities have co-existed ever since and while other places of learning tend to be regarded with contempt by the 'Oxbridge' establishment, the two universities hold each other in grudging respect. The term 'Oxbridge' was only coined in 1849, when William Thackeray had the protagonist of his novel *Pendennis* attend (and fail)

'St. Boniface College, Oxbridge'; it took more than a century before the term made its way into common usage.

The growth of both universities depended for a long time on the good will of the Church; many colleges were founded in the late Middle Ages by rich bishops. They both survived the dissolution of the monasteries under Henry VIII because they received special dispensation through royal decrees. In return, both had to be loyal to the Church of England; Catholics, Jews and dissenters were not allowed to study here until the nineteenth century.

The system at both universities is different from what we foreigners may know from our own countries; rather than having one unified institution, Oxbridge is made up of a loose association of its colleges, which are self-governed and fiercely independent. The size of the universities is quite similar: Oxford has 35 colleges for just over 20,000 students, Cambridge has 31 colleges for slightly under 20,000 students. In both cities, there are quite a large number of other colleges and educational institutions, which do not form part of the universities, but bask in the glory of their location's reputation.

Both Oxford and Cambridge make it very hard for people to get in; thousands of applicants are rejected every year. Going to a top public school obviously helps – both universities are criticised regularly for being biased against applicants from 'ordinary' state schools and have now been forced to reserve a certain percentage of their places for these less privileged students.

Compared to studying at a top Ivy League university in the USA, the fees at Oxbridge look laughable: tuition fees at entry level are £9,000 per year for British and EU students; for overseas students this goes up to £18,000 in some subjects. Grants and loans are available for those who cannot afford such fees.

What is the big difference between the two? I could not say. As a rule of thumb, Oxford has always been stronger in the humanities, while Cambridge made its name in the sciences. But who would argue the quality of either of them, when they have educated people such as John Wycliffe and John Wesley; Oliver Cromwell and Winston Churchill; Isaac Newton, Charles Darwin and Ernest Rutherford, and even a raft of writers from Lord Byron to John Betjeman and Salman Rushdie? Cambridge tops Oxford when it comes to Soviet-era spies: Kim Philby, Anthony Blunt and Guy Burgess were all Cambridge men. But I doubt the university counts that among its achievements.

Some of the differences are down to semantics; in Oxford you study in a 'tutorial', in Cambridge it is a 'supervision'; your Oxford doctorate is a 'D.Phil', the Cambridge version is a 'Ph.D'. The biggest difference may be the position from which you steer your punt: in Oxford, you navigate the Isis (which is the Thames, only by a poetic name) from the bow; in Cambridge you try to avoid falling into the Cam steering from the stern.

Henry James suggested an answer to the question of which

university is better when he said: 'If Oxford were not the finest thing in England, the case would be clearer for Cambridge.'*

I'll leave you with that thought.

---

* Henry James, *Collected Travel Writing. Great Britain and America*. New York, 1993, p.210

King's Cross, London

Where we will not board a train,
but we will join a queue, just for the fun of it

When we were at school, we learnt that politeness is the most important quality in a proper English person. We learnt that people will constantly say 'beg your pardon' or 'sorry' or 'thank you'. Gentlemen will open doors for ladies, and the English will happily join a queue wherever they can find one.

Well, in everyday life you will encounter a certain level of civility that tends to make life easier. If somebody steps on your foot on the underground, they may apologise. In the shops, the lady at the cash register may still hand over your change saying 'here you are, luv'. And sometimes even a taxi driver might say 'thank you' when you give him a tip. That is quite nice.

But you should not overestimate these things. Especially in the cities, it is more common today to hear a grunting noise when you hand over your money in a shop or on a bus. Entering the Tube in peak traffic, all gloves are off and what might have looked like some sort of orderly queue quickly dissolves into a shove-and-thrust as soon as the doors open. And when you order a beer in a pub, people tend not to wait their turn but to cut in at any given opportunity. Some may call these examples of everyday behaviour 'continental' and blame falling standards on TV and the continuous influx of foreigners bringing their own ideas of behaviour with them. Let's settle upon the old classic: the times, they are a-changing.

But of course, there are still a number of the old rituals: meeting and greeting people is as ritualised as ever. The dreaded greeting 'How do you do,' might sound a tad formal today, but as long as you are not being introduced to a pal's pal in a pub, it is still quite common. And as has been the case since time immemorial, the person stretching out his hand and inquiring after your well-being could not care less about it. Whatever you may wish to say in this moment, do not give a brief description of your recent colonoscopy or relate your worries about the recently discovered subsidence in your house. Just take the person's hand, shake it and answer 'How do you do?' yourself. If you can muster a smile, do it, but it's not strictly necessary. Neither you nor your new acquaintance have given or received a proper answer to the introductory question – but that's alright, nobody really expects you to.

How do you continue? There is only one possible way: make a remark about the weather. As Samuel Johnson pointed out: 'It is commonly observed, that when two Englishmen meet, their first talk is of the weather.' Just as in 'How do you do?' a remark such as 'Nice day, isn't it,' has got nothing to do with the actual meaning of the words. We all know that

English weather doesn't have many hurricanes or other stirring tales to tell, but that's not the point. The weather is merely a means to get a conversation going, an ice-breaker that establishes a common ground on which both parties to the conversation can continue in relative safety. And with the weather as a trigger, the conversation will most certainly lurch into full flow.

The English do shake hands – not often, but yes, they do. But they are not huggers. Ladies may greet each other with just the slightest imitation of a hug and a couple of kisses blown into the air. That's about it. That said, it is true that behaviour is changing and good friends might greet each other with a bear hug, at least amongst the younger generations in the cities. Try and hug a farmer and he will almost certainly set his dogs on you.

Formal etiquette is still observed in England, especially when it comes to dress codes. Nowhere in Europe will you need to turn up at events wearing 'black tie' (that's your dinner jacket, tuxedo, if you are American) as often as in England. Most of the time, your invitation will tell you what's expected of you, as long as you are a man. I have never seen an invitation which gave a prescription for ladies' wear – probably because of the working assumption that females will always instinctively know what to do, while men, if left to their own devices, would turn up to the Royal Garden Party wearing jeans and a T-shirt. With formal wear, you don't even need to own these things: there are lots of shops who will happily lend you the full garb, even if you need the full formal getup, including a top hat.

I have always found English formal etiquette rather user-friendly: if you follow the rules, you will know what to wear, where to put your hand during dinner, who is supposed to introduce whom – it takes away the awkwardness and the headache of worrying about what to do and how to do it. And never forget to write a 'Thank You' letter after an evening at a private home. Even if the food was awful, the wine corked and the host's little daughter Jemima spilt her soup over your pants, tell them what a lovely evening you had. It may seem archaic – but it's nice. And next time around, you can happily pretend to be otherwise engaged.

'Manners' are an altogether different thing. Here, the guiding principle is respect. It is a matter of respect for other people, whether or not you plonk your feet onto the opposite seat when you are on the Underground (a big no-no), or whether you let a door swing into the face of the person following you into a building.

And, of course, there still is the ancient tradition of queuing. George Mikes, who came to England from Hungary in the 1930s, described queuing as a national passion, and even today, queues are important, especially when it comes to the social psychology of the English. Queue-jumping is regarded as a severe breach of etiquette, even deeply immoral.

In some areas of everyday life, English politeness and good manners still work very well: road traffic is one of them.

Whether you are driving in France, Italy or Germany, you will encounter the hidden side of your pleasant neighbour as soon as he sits behind a steering wheel; the road becomes his and you suddenly morph from person into obstacle. In England, this hardly happens. For whatever reason, the English are relaxed and forthcoming drivers. Even in deepest inner London, where the 'cool kids' drive around with earth-shattering noise coming out of giant boom boxes, they might endanger the well-being of your ear drums and insult your taste in music – but they will hardly ever use their horns or flash their lights, and they will happily and patiently stop at zebra crossings. England has one of the lowest rates of traffic mortality in the world. I like to think that this is due, at least in part, to deeply ingrained good manners.

Never complain: the English hate nothing more than being confrontational. A complaint is regarded as extremely bad form and it will easily get you identified as an 'alien'. The English go by the maxim 'mustn't grumble', even though everyday life gives them ample opportunity for grumbling, be it the crumbling transport infrastructure, the horrendous prices and fees you have to pay for whatever you wish to have done, or your plumber's botched repair works. 'Take it on the chin', 'grin and bear it', 'such is life' – just as the Inuit have 70 different words for snow, the English seem to have at least as many expressions they can use to avoid complaining.

Good manners and politeness can also be a convenient

tactical weapon. Not being confrontational easily translates into infuriating dithering in business matters; it is very difficult to get a decisive answer from an English business partner, and even then, it is safer not to take anything for granted until it has been written down and the contract signed. Try to get someone to call you back – in 99 per cent of all cases, the call will be promised but never made. And if you happen to work for an English company, your boss will hardly ever let you know if something is wrong. Even if you make a really big mistake, your boss will be at pains to let you know that he is not *actually* criticising you. It would be unwise not to take this non-confrontational approach seriously: English bosses love to fire people and they do it with particular glee. Quite often, the person who has just been made redundant will be given a bin liner and 30 minutes to clear his desk, with security guards overseeing the proceedings.

Good manners help the English to conquer the trials and tribulations of everyday life. Controlling your emotions and cracking a joke also helps – we will deal with these instruments later. The anthropologist Kate Fox speaks about the 'social disease' that haunts the English, which seems to be a mixture of autism and agoraphobia. Never standing out, always conforming to what is expected of you is an easy way to deal with this 'dis-ease'. And of course, it helps to avoid unpleasant truths.

Eton, Berkshire

A place to learn what makes a man

Oh, the playing fields of Eton. No other school has produced so many politicians and captains of industry, diplomats and city crooks. They are all gentlemen, Eton gentlemen. And they all have a very 'stiff upper lip'.

While Italians are famous for singing and Americans for praying, the English lead the world in keeping mute in the face of adversity. The 'stiff upper lip' seems to be the most important part of an Englishman's anatomy, and is one of the very few you may mention in polite society. The expression comes from America, but it fits no other nations as it fits the English. You may call it cold-blooded, being oblivious, or simply being a bit thick.

You may recall the wonderful movie *Around the World in 80 Days*, with David Niven playing the gentleman traveller, Phileas Fogg. His portrayal is the epitome of the 'stiff upper lip'; whatever destiny throws at him, he keeps his cool, while his French man-servant Passepartout suffers one nervous fit after the other. Phileas Fogg, a creation of the French writer Jules Verne, is of course a product of a 'public school education', which is obviously accessible to the whole public, as long as you can cough up enough cash.

Public schools were the purveyors of gentlemen who served their country in industry and administration, especially in the colonies. The educational principle was very down to earth: a good dose of Greek, Latin and History, plus a lot of sports. Teachers had their fun, too: just set tough academic tasks for the strong and big boys, and select the small, weak ones for rugby and boxing – hey presto, what a lot of pleasurable suffering one can cause with very little effort! The food served in these schools was also part of the educational experience – after a couple of years at a public school, the proud administrators of the English colonies could not find the natives' food too abhorrent. To add to these ingenious educational principles, the birch was quick at hand to deal out savage beatings, mostly for no particular reason. If the boys took their punishment without flinching or batting an eyelid, one knew that the educational aims had been achieved.

Pedagogic ideas may have changed a bit in recent years, but you can trust the public schools still to adhere to the ideology behind the ancient tradition. Just look at the school uniforms that Eton prescribes, with the stiff white collars and tailcoats – it takes some 'stiff upper lip' to carry off such a getup without falling into a fit of embarrassed giggles. Other public schools have adopted a more relaxed code with blazers and ties, but this second-oldest public school (it was founded in 1440, half a century after the arch rival, Winchester) is defiantly sticking to its guns in this respect. After all, if the parents cough up around £30,000 annually, their sons may well be expected to endure a little suffering.

We foreigners may think that not showing emotion is not a clever way to go. In England, it is the ideal of gentlemanly behaviour. He who shows his emotions doesn't only ruin his own reputation; he also embarrasses others into caring for the sentimental wreck. As silly as this may sound, there is some reasoning behind it: there is no such thing as a disaster – it is only made disastrous by your inadequate reactions and sentiments. It's called stoicism.

Rudyard Kipling, winner of the Nobel Prize for Literature in 1907, has written the most touching advice for the aspiring gentleman:

If

If you can keep your head when all about you
Are losing theirs and blaming it on you,
If you can trust yourself when all men doubt you,
But make allowance for their doubting too;
If you can wait and not be tired by waiting,
Or being lied about, don't deal in lies,
Or being hated, don't give way to hating,
And yet don't look too good, nor talk too wise:

If you can dream – and not make dreams your master;
If you can think – and not make thoughts your aim;

If you can meet with Triumph and Disaster
And treat those two impostors just the same;
If you can bear to hear the truth you've spoken
Twisted by knaves to make a trap for fools,
Or watch the things you gave your life to, broken,
And stoop and build 'em up with worn-out tools:

If you can make one heap of all your winnings
And risk it on one turn of pitch-and-toss,
And lose, and start again at your beginnings
And never breathe a word about your loss;
If you can force your heart and nerve and sinew
To serve your turn long after they are gone,
And so hold on when there is nothing in you
Except the Will which says to them: 'Hold on!'

If you can talk with crowds and keep your virtue,
Or walk with kings – nor lose the common touch,
If neither foes nor loving friends can hurt you,
If all men count with you, but none too much;
If you can fill the unforgiving minute
With sixty seconds' worth of distance run,
Yours is the Earth and everything that's in it,
And – which is more – you'll be a Man, my son!

The Collected Poems of Rudyard Kipling,
Wordsworth Poetry Library, 1999

Stiff upper lip has always been a lifeline for the English – just think of the dark times during the Second World War, when the people in the cities had to endure the Nazi bombing raids. Churchill's rousing speeches and, of course, the refusal of the royal family to leave London during the Blitz, were public demonstrations of the nation's stiff upper lip, which helped the English to withstand the onslaught.

But, of course, the times are changing – since the death of Princess Diana in 1997, the nation has begun to indulge in public manifestations of emotion. This modern-day sentimentality has been fuelled by the tabloid press – probing into public people's private sentiments and exposing them to a lecherous readership has long been the basis of their business. Be it the divorce of a popular sports star, the illness of an actor's wife, or the death of a Z-list celebrity: today, the nation's upper lip wobbles in tune to the headlines of the red-tops.

Soho, London

Humour it may be, but no laughing matter

D ear reader, I am German. As such, I do not have a sense of humour. That's bad news. But I have worse news: if you are from France, Holland, Sweden, Spain or any other non-English country, you don't have a sense of humour either. It's even worse if you are American; you don't even understand the basic concept of humour (despite your brilliant TV sitcoms, which the English simply adore). There is no need to argue about it. It's what the English say. And they should know – they do have a sense of humour. That's what they say.

Humour is big business in England; every day of the week, you can attend stand up comedy acts in any major town, with Soho (London's traditional entertainment district) being the epicentre of the movement.

English humour comes in various forms, but the one we admire most does not easily lend itself to description or definition. It is the wordplay, the quick exchange of semi-sentences and seemingly unconnected asides that generates humour. It indulges in a certain 'blackness' – death and suffering are commonly used to drive a comic point home. And it is often outright xenophobic: I remember a comedy quiz on BBC Radio 4 where the participants had to say what they would do if they saw a car lying in a ditch. One participant said he would take a look and drive on if the people inside were German. The audience collapsed laughing. Germans, French, Belgians, the Irish, the Americans – they are all the butt of savage jokes. If you dare lift your finger to complain, it only proves that you have no sense of humour. At least you cannot do jokes about black people anymore, as Margaret Thatcher's daughter found out after she was overheard cracking a racist joke – she was immediately relieved of her duties as a panellist on BBC shows.

The BBC is one of the most important sponsors for comedic talent. Since its inception in the 1920s, the broadcaster has always produced a healthy dose of radio and TV comedy and has helped to develop the talents of such outstanding acts as Monty Python, which of course owes its existence to *The Goon Show*, which infected a generation of young people (including Prince Charles) with the giggles from the 1950s onwards. Not a day goes by without at least 30 minutes of radio comedy, and when you go to the BBC on the internet, you can find a plethora of archived material.

Much of the famous English humour is not different from what we know on the continent: go to any English seaside resort and look at the abundance of smutty postcards – just what you find in Spanish, Italian or German resorts. Or look at the famous 'Knock, knock' jokes, such as this one:

Knock, Knock!
Who's there?
Juno.
Juno who?
Juno that I'm out here, right?

I don't find this too funny. But that's because I, being German, don't have a sense of humour.

Another indigenous form of English humour grips the nation around Christmas: Panto fever. 'Pantomimes' are a theatrical genre you won't find in any other country. Most of them are variations of fairy tale classics, such as *Puss in Boots* or *Cinderella*. As a rule, the acting has to be as bad as possible. Men dress up in women's clothes, there is lots of sexual innuendo, kicking of backsides and throwing of things. There is always the fight between rich and poor, with the rich guys always being very evil and the poor ones as good as saints. The typical dialogue in a panto goes: 'You can't do that!' – 'Oh yes, I can!' – 'Oh no, you can't!' – 'Oh yes, I can!' – and so on, for as long as the audience is willing to join in the shouting match. If you really want to encounter the English in their most un-'stiff upper lippy' mode, go to a panto!

I have said that I am not a big fan of the 'Knock, knock' school of English humour. But this basic and often very silly genre uses the most important ingredient of English humour: the pun. Hardly any other language offers this instrument, which is the result of the historic mix-up of languages and inconsistent orthographic rules. When you add these two, you end up with an endless number of 'homonyms' – words sounding different, but being spelt alike; and 'homographs' – words sounding alike but being spelt differently. 'Sun' and 'son' is a good example, or 'to lie' in bed and 'to lie', as in not telling the truth.

The pun is a tricky customer; Dr Johnson, the sage of the eighteenth century and compiler of the first English dictionary, called it the lowest form of humour. Fortunately, William Shakespeare lived long before Johnson and did not know that his extensive punning would one day be frowned upon. If you don't make allowance for puns, you will not be able to understand the full meaning of many of Shakespeare's plays and sonnets. I have been told that the Bard used about 3,000 puns in his works – I have not counted them, but I would not be surprised if that were true. Even in his darkest tragedies, Shakespeare applied moments of 'comic relief' to allow his audience to take a deep breath and clear their minds before plunging even deeper into the tragic abyss.

Despite Johnson's verdict, the pun has remained a mainstay of comedic writing and acting. Oscar Wilde used it to quip 'Immanuel doesn't pun, he Kant.'

As a rule, hilarity only ensues if a sentence leads to something unexpected; the surprising end of a joke relieves the tension that has built up during the narration. This is where English word play rules; apart from the puns, it is the grammatical structure of the language that enables the narrator to hold back with the surprising resolution. It works best in grotesque situations. One of my favourites goes like this: 'A monkey in the zoo sits in his cage, shaking his head over two books: the Bible and Darwin's *Origin of Species*. When a fellow monkey inquires what it is that's puzzling him, he responds: "I don't know whether I am my brother's keeper, or my keeper's brother."' Or: 'Three windows argue about their favourite band. They can only agree on one thing: they all hate The Doors.' Or, even more absurd: 'A road and an avenue are in a bar. A good-looking lady comes in. "Watch out," says the road, "She's a complete cyclepath."'

A sense of humour is the key to almost everything in England, starting with the kind of humour you have to display when yet another cowboy builder, electrician or plumber has turned your house into a disaster zone. As a rule, no politician can survive without it, which is one reason why Margaret Thatcher became a hated figure so quickly. Politicians regard comedy panel shows on TV and radio as perfect opportunities to present themselves to the public, even though they know that they will be given a brutal ribbing by their fellow panellists, who tend to be sharp and hard-nosed professional comedians. Both Ken Livingstone and Boris Johnson, successive mayors of London, are brilliant comedic performers and both used comedy panel shows as staging posts for their political comebacks.

In Europe and the United States, a politician taking part in a comedy show is always at risk of being mistaken for an intellectual lightweight. Nobody in England would think that. In fact, when you watch the better English stand-up acts or listen to comedic radio shows, you will find that they require an extraordinary amount of wit, intellect and learning. If a public figure can brave the spears and arrows of such enemies, he is seen as a hero.

In politics, jokes are used as a tool of attack. This is an accepted part of the daily heave-ho of parliamentary politics, but in private conversation, it is not considered good form to crack jokes at the expense of others. Self-deprecation is the way to go – if you have to joke about anybody's bad taste in clothes, it had better be your own. If you want to mock somebody who could not whack a nail on its head if his life depended on it, it has to be you.

Freud explained that a joke is a sublimation of the killer instinct and he was, of course, right: nothing – short of murder – destroys an opponent as radically as a good sharp joke. The English humour is more geared towards the defensive function; it helps keep intruders into your privacy at bay. Just like the ideal of the 'stiff upper lip', humour serves as a handy way to avoid revealing your emotions. Crises, anxiety and shyness – all these can be tucked away in your inner safety box as long as you can still joke about things. Once again, a joke in times of distress does not mean that the joker is dim; maybe the English have simply given up on trying to overcome existential doubts in the face of the absurdity of life. Even the absurdest jokes may just be signs of rude sanity.

When in doubt, the English can always revert to laughing at the failure of foreigners to pronounce obscure place names correctly or understand the underlying meaning of a conversation. The popularity in England of the following table, which went viral on the internet recently, just goes to show how funny the English find our inability to wade through the layers of non-confrontational language and subtle irony to decipher what is really being said.

What the English say	What the English mean	What others understand
I hear what you say	I disagree and do not want to discuss it further	He accepts my point of view
With the greatest respect ...	I think you are an idiot	He is listening to me
That's not bad	That's good	That's poor
That is a very brave proposal	You are insane	He thinks I have courage
Quite good	A bit disappointing	Quite good
I would suggest ...	Do it or be prepared to justify yourself	Think about the idea, but do what you like
Oh, incidentally/by the way	The primary purpose of our discussion is ...	That is not very important
I was a bit disappointed that	I am annoyed that	It doesn't really matter
Very interesting	That is clearly nonsense	They are impressed
I'll bear it in mind	I've forgotten it already	They will probably do it
I'm sure it's my fault	It's your fault	Why do they think it was their fault?

What the English say	What the English mean	What others understand
You must come for dinner	It's not an invitation, I'm just being polite	I will get an invitation soon
I almost agree	I don't agree at all	He's not far from agreement
I only have a few minor comments	Please re-write completely	He has found a few typos
Could we consider some other options	I don't like your idea	They have not yet decided

Which only leaves one question: why do the English (much like the Americans) always have those idiotic tapes of canned laughter played throughout their comedies? Does it mean that they wouldn't get the jokes without them? I think we should be told!

Windsor Castle, Berkshire

*In which we are obediently amused
by the Windsor Soap Opera*

Humour certainly helps to tackle the issue of the English royals. Writing in this, the 60th year of Queen Elizabeth's blessed reign, we have to take the short trip up the Thames towards Windsor and take a look at Her Majesty's most formidable residence. Windsor Castle is the world's largest and oldest inhabited castle, providing ample space for the royal corgis to run around. Eton is just down the road, there is a royal chapel, a great park (which, with stunning originality, is called 'Windsor Great Park') and, of course, there are also all the fixtures a proper medieval castle requires – turrets and moats, stables and servants' quarters and a well-stocked gift shop to serve the tourists who are actually paying for the upkeep of the whole thing.

Tourism may not have been the first thing that came to the mind of William the Conqueror when he found the place. The ground on which he built his castle was within easy reach of his residence in the Tower of London, had entertaining hunting grounds and from its position it would dominate the surroundings, as so many castles built in Norman times do.

Like the Tower, Windsor Castle started its life as a wooden fortress and William's successors, enjoying the pleasant surroundings, kept on building for centuries. Today, the grounds of the castle cover some 100,000 square metres. It is divided into two major 'wards', with the lower one housing the royal chapel and the upper one the royal chambers and grand halls used for official occasions. St. George's Hall, built by Edward III who had most of the present buildings erected from 1350, is perhaps the most magnificent among them – a purpose-built hall for the Knights of the Garter, the most noble order he founded when a lovely lady lost her garter, or so the story goes. The aspect from the Thames is dominated by the 'Round Tower' which, in homage to the sacred traditions of English craftsmen, is more elliptical than circular. From 1390, Windsor Castle had a remarkable overseer of its building works: Geoffrey Chaucer, the author of *The Canterbury Tales*.

All this building work resulted in a splendid residence, much to the pleasure of Oliver Cromwell, who encouraged his soldiers to loot the royal treasure to make up for unpaid wages.

I already mentioned Windsor Great Park, which is partly accessible to the public. Some years ago, Prince Andrew came up with the idea of converting the park into a golf club. Fortunately, the Queen forbade it. A tour of the royal chambers reveals part of the Queen's huge art collection – it comprises more pictures than the collections of the Tate and National galleries combined. A visit to Queen Mary's Dolls' House, the world's largest, completes the tour.

Tourists are allowed almost free run of Windsor Castle –
thanks mainly to the great fire which destroyed almost 100
rooms in 1992. The Queen consented to the opening of the
castle to generate the cash needed for repairs and renovation.
It worked: no tax payer's money was needed.

Of course, Windsor Castle is immediately identified with
the present royal family who even adopted the name, when
being called 'Saxe-Coburg-Gotha' became uncool during
the First World War. We foreigners assume that the English
like their royals, because we always see Her Majesty's subjects
going into a national frenzy on royal occasions such as weddings and funerals. Well, most English have a certain respect
for the Queen, and probably even more so with each year that
she manages to soldier on. For most of the rest of the royal
family, there is a mixture of public loathing and indifference.

Year after year, surveys show an astonishing support for
the Royals: 75 per cent of Her Majesty's subjects wish to keep
the monarchy going, and only 18 per cent long for a republic,
even though a whopping 64 per cent think they should not
receive as much money through the civil list as they do today.*
But one has to put this into perspective: the state subsidies to
the Queen and her family, including grants for the upkeep of
the residences and travel costs, run to a tad over £32 million
per year, which means that the monarchy comes to an annual

---

* Ipsos MORI Research Archive: Monarchy/Royal Family Trends –
Monarchy v Republic 1993–2011

outlay for every person in the kingdom of less than 50 pence – you don't even get a download on your iPod for that. And given the fact that the annual profits of around £200 million from the Crown Estate go into the Treasury's coffers, the royals are good business for the country.

Approval ratings for the family, and the Queen personally, have been rather stable over the past few years – a significant dip in 1997, at the time of Diana's death, was followed by a steady increase. Since 2009, when large-scale fraud, benefit-abuse and various other nefarious activities committed by Members of Parliament came to light, the Queen's approval rating has soared significantly; and the royal wedding in 2011 saw to it that the positive ratings reached an all-time high.

Wills & Kate, whose wedding had billions of people worldwide glued to the television may well be the breath of fresh air that the monarchy needed after Diana's death. The young couple fulfil their public duties faultlessly; William's continued service in the RAF emphasises the seriousness of the young man who will be king one day. Even William's younger brother Harry, who had been paparazzi-fodder for years, seems to have got his act together; one does not really miss reports about his nights out clubbing or his infamous appearance at a costume party dressed up in full Nazi regalia.

Even if she had negative ratings, the Queen would not need to worry too much: the monarchy's position is clad in iron by the law. It is a crime to call for the abolition of the monarchy; culprits are liable to sentences ranging as far as life imprisonment or deportation. In 2001, the High Court refused to even scrutinise the Treason Felony Act of 1848, which had been introduced at a time when liberal and republican movements thrived on the continent; it outlaws demands for the introduction of a republic. If you like writing letters, you better beware, too: putting the stamp bearing the monarch's head upside down on the envelope is regarded as an act of treason.

In any case, the royal family may well pay for its upkeep through the enormous revenues generated by royal-related tourism. For each visiting foreigner, a brief look at Buckingham Palace, the Queen's London 'home' is *de rigueur*, as is a trip to Windsor and to the memorials to Diana, the 'Queen of Hearts' who was the only person to have been able to jeopardise the Queen's position, if only after her untimely death.

But what do we make of the rest of the family? Royal marriages have never been the same as ours. But the shenanigans of the Queen's sister Margaret, of Charles & Diana, Andrew & Fergie, of Anne and her various husbands, as well as some of the youngest generation, point to a mighty abundance of testosterone and a hearty lack of decorum. Edward and his as-yet undivorced marriage do not make things better: the Queen's youngest son landed his family in the soft soap through his wacky idea of taking part in a 'Royal Knockout' show on television and later got even more egg on his face when his film production company broke the general 'off limits' policy the English press applied to coverage of Prince William while he was at the University of St Andrews. His wife, a hearty blonde lass going by the wonderful Welsh name Sophie Rhys-Jones, had to abandon her career in PR after it transpired that she had told details of the royals' family life to a nasty journalist posing as a rich potential client.

Not much later, Sarah Ferguson (Fergie) stumbled into a similar trap: she offered exclusive access to her ex-husband Prince Andrew – for the small fee of £500,000. When the story broke, she argued that she had been drunk at the time. How Prince Philip must have wished for the times of Henry VIII returning, if only for one day!

Well, the Windsor soap opera is likely to continue. Nobody believes the Queen is considering stepping down, and Charles is unlikely to step aside in favour of his son. You don't live a public life for 60 years to chicken out at the crucial moment. The motto in the Prince's coat of arms says '*Ich Dien*' – 'I Serve', and this is what Charles will most certainly do. Architects and industrialists will not like this king: he has made a name for himself by yammering on about buildings and ecology. His own endeavours in these fields are not a good omen; his model village, Poundbury, is the archetype of non-sustainable development, with middle-density suburban housing in a setting without an urban centre to cling to, it just feels odd and not very well thought through. It's twee. Noddy houses use up an enormous space for very few people. If we all lived in such places, the world would soon no longer have any green spaces left.

As I said, the royal family's position is rather secure. The only possible threat may come from the republican quarters of the News International media conglomerate, whose proprietor (the now notorious) Rupert Murdoch rumbled on somberly in an interview with *The Times* some years ago; having endured five hours in a VIP area to watch Queen Elizabeth's golden jubilee celebrations, he said that the monarchy might not survive a monarch who got lippy about politics and such things.* A clear warning to Prince Charles if ever there was one; and a clear reminder of Lenin's warning that 'all over the world, wherever there are capitalists, freedom of the press means freedom to buy up newspapers, to buy writers, to bribe, buy and fake "public opinion" for the benefit of the bourgeoisie.'†

---

* 2002 interview by James Harding in *The Times*, quoted in Dan Sabbagh: 'Murdoch to face new grilling as newspaper families are called to account'. The *Guardian*, 21 April 2012.

† 'Letter to G. Myasnikov'. *Lenin's Collected Works*, vol. 32. Moscow, 1965.

Fleet Street, London

*We miss our colleagues and pass the time
reading the papers*

As a rule, journalists don't do romantic stuff. We are a tough, hard-nosed bunch of go-getters. We are underpaid, but incorruptible; we are moody, but we have a heart of gold; we may not be the best family people, but we are loyal to our pubs and wine bars. And we have a church, St. Bride's, just a couple of metres off Fleet Street. Inside, you will find a small museum of the history of printing and a number of memorials to journalists, some of whom died in action. The church stands in the place occupied by St. Bridget's, which, in the sixth century, was the first-ever church to be built in London; it was destroyed by the Great Fire of 1666.

St. Bride's is not a big church and architecturally, you may find many more interesting buildings. But it is one of the last remnants of a time gone by, a time when England's journalistic heart beat along the 'Street of Shame' and reliable boozers such as 'Ye Olde Cheshire Cheese' were hotbeds of gossip and information.

England was the first European country where a vibrant media scene developed, following the introduction of the printing press in the late fifteenth century. England was also the first European country to grant press freedom (impeded to this day by savage libel laws) in 1695, and a copyright law that transferred intellectual property from printers to authors.

Almost from the beginning, Fleet Street became the centre of the new industry, with many printers setting up shop, producing books and pamphlets galore. The first English newspaper, the *Daily Courant* was published here on 11 March 1702. The end for Fleet Street began in 1986, when Rupert Murdoch's News International company, publishers of newspapers such as the *Sun*, *The Times* and *The Sunday Times* (his Sunday paper the *News of the World* was closed down following the phone hacking scandal in 2011) led the exodus of the industry to cheaper and logistically easier premises elsewhere; Reuters, the news agency, was the last media company to leave in 2005.

So, Fleet Street is a bit of a memory lane today, but the basic characteristics of the English press have not changed. They still thrive on politics and class conflict, love and scandal in celebrity circles and of course, the really important stuff in life, like the new hair-do of a footballer's wife.

Nowhere in Europe do we find a gutter press as vicious as here, nowhere else are politicians butchered as assiduously. H.L. Mencken's old adage that the only proper relationship between a journalist and a politician resembles that between a dog and a tree is put into daily practice, much to the benefit of the country.

Some years ago, the Tory MP Neil Hamilton was found to

have taken bribes for asking questions and giving speeches on particular topics in parliament. He denied all charges, was convicted in court and has had to eke out a living as a C-list celebrity ever since. Jonathan Aitken, a former minister of state in the Ministry of Defence, denied reports by the *Guardian* and Channel 4 that he had met Arab arms dealers in a Paris hotel. He threatened to defend his honour with the 'sword of truth', and ended up 'doing porridge' for perjury. He found the time to hand over his possessions to his wife, divorce her and thus escape having to pay damages. He found the Lord in prison, he says. Many observers also fondly remember the perjury trial against Jeffrey Archer, the super-bestselling thriller writer and Tory MP who was found guilty of perjury and sent to chokey – his career also came to a crunching halt thanks to the tabloids. And when the big expenses scandal broke in 2009, exposing dozens of MPs and ministers as cheats and frauds, it was of course the media which had dug up the whole thing.

Daily parliamentary sketches are a speciality of the English press; this is where the best and brightest writers find their turf. They take particular pleasure in puncturing the hot air balloons of today's political lingo. They may sometimes go for the silly mode: calling Roy Hattersley 'Fattersley' is a bit juvenile; on the other hand, the former Tory minister Michael Heseltine wore his nickname 'Tarzan' with great pride.

Simon Hoggart, the veteran sketch writer for the *Guardian* is my particular favourite, with his loving care about the real meaning of what is said in parliament. When Chancellor

George Osborne announced that the minimum pension age might be increased, Hoggart called it the 'they shall not grow old' budget. Good fun was also to be head at one Prime Minister's Questions, which led Hoggart to write: 'When the PM feels the heat, he does what Indiana Jones does and pulls out a gun. Or, to be precise, a rhetorical question.'*

Hoggart and his colleagues are what might be called 'waste management specialists'. They dissect the flummery of daily politics in a way that appeals to weary, but intelligent readers who don't expect too much good to come out of parliament. Once again, this tried and tested instrument, English humour, helps to make life a bit more agreeable.

The other end of the scale is occupied by the gutter press, which makes a living out of misinformation and hypocrisy. They ardently exploit national stereotypes, especially when it comes to the French and Germans and don't see how the high pitched headline-screaming about the alleged sex-crazedness of teenagers and the picture of a naked lady on the same page might just be seen as a bit of a double standard. At their best, these mass market papers have unveiled numerous sex scandals, corruption and fraud and have been ruthless in exposing politicians, footballers and business leaders. At their worst, these papers have destroyed lives and reputations at the drop of a hat. When questioned about their actions, journalists from these papers will normally tell you that it is 'all in good

---

* The *Guardian*, 29 February 2012.

spirit' and 'a bit of fun' – but it really isn't. Sometimes their actions have tragic consequences: think of Princess Diana's death in Paris, when her car, pursued by paparazzi, crashed in a tunnel. The gutter press joined the howling sentimentality and beatified a woman about whom they had said only a week before her death, that if her IQ was just a few points lower she would need watering.

When it comes to politics, the tabloids in particular wield a power that might be seen as unsavoury. Of course it is only sensible for politicians to think about the media's reaction to new proposals and policies but at times it seems that papers such as the *Sun*, the *Daily Mail* or the *Mirror* have succeeded in dictating policies to the politicians. No politician can openly argue for joining the Eurozone without having his teeth kicked out by the media; whether it is social reform, immigration or drugs policies – if you get the media's gander up, you do so at your own peril. Stanley Baldwin, the Prime Minister in the 1920s, said of the media: 'They look for power, power without responsibility – the prerogative of the harlot through the ages.'

The real crisis for this part of the media arrived in 2011 when it was revealed that the *News of the World* and other papers had illegally hacked into the mobile phones of celebrities, politicians and victims of crime; there were also allegations of bribery and collusion involving various police forces. Almost 50 people were arrested; the *News of the World* was closed down as a first consequence of the scandal, only to be replaced by a Sunday edition of its sister publication, the *Sun* a couple of months later. The scandal led to a parliamentary enquiry, which was still going on at the time of writing. Even though I would not speculate about the outcome, it seems likely that the legal framework governing the working of the press will be tightened significantly.

As far back as 1799, in the famous 'Cuthell's Case', Lord Chief Justice Kenyon argued that 'the liberty of the press is dear to England; the licentiousness of the press is odious to England: the liberty of it can never be so well protected as by beating down the licentiousness.' There is a real danger that the press as such will become muzzled as a result of the wrongdoings of overzealous gutter hacks, especially if you look at the outdated and fearsome libel legislation that has made England the venue of choice for any potentate to take legal action against criticism. The press may have been given its freedom in 1695, but this freedom has been restricted by these libel laws. Until late in the nineteenth century, truth was not recognised as a defence in libel cases; in fact, even if the media reported a political scandal correctly, it did not protect them from legal retribution – the greater the truth, the greater the libel, was the doctrine upheld by the courts. Parliament has been made aware of the problems created by the present libel system – whether it will act to ensure press freedom is another matter entirely.

Ambridge, Nowhereshire

*A place in the air, where the waves
are the voice of the world*

No, you need not try to find Ambridge on a map – it is a fictitious village created by the BBC more than 60 years ago. Since 1 January 1951, *The Archers* have populated the airwaves, telling the story of a farming family. From their accents you can tell that Ambridge may be located in the West Country; but its true location for many decades has been in the radio listeners' hearts.

The BBC was founded in 1922 and has set the standard for public, non-commercial radio and television ever since. It has been the blueprint for broadcasting companies in many countries. It has always upheld aims such as strengthening democracy and civil society, promoting education and creativity and of course, hammering home the British view of things to listeners and viewers around the world.

The Archers is a prime example of the best the BBC has to offer, and by this I do not imply that the series is particularly original, entertaining or clever. On the contrary, the daily dish of intrigue and petty squabbles, love, jealousy, illness, death and birth is as banal as it gets. But, possibly because it has been around for such a long time, *The Archers* has become an indispensable part of everyday life. The reason why I admire the programme is its unwavering dedication to its cause: informing and educating the farming community.

Following the Second World War, agricultural production in England did not perform at its optimum; young men from farming communities who had been drafted into the military did not return to their old jobs following demobilisation but preferred better paid jobs in industry. The situation deteriorated to such a level that rationing of staples such as potatoes and bread, which had not been necessary during the war, was introduced after the fighting had ended.

Sponsored by the Ministry of Agriculture, *The Archers* was launched to bring new impetus into the farming community, telling them about new methods of farming, new technology and financial aid that were being made available. Instead of doing this through a series of highly informative but possibly very dull broadcasts, the programme makers chose the fictional form and came up with a tremendous success: every weekday at 7:05 p.m., the nation tunes in to *The Archers* on Radio 4; and to the repeat at 2:05 p.m. the following day... and even to the *Archers Omnibus*, which is broadcast every weekend. The daily average of five million listeners means that the recipe still works today – gene technology and environmental concerns, pension schemes and cancer screening, the outbreak of epidemics and new government schemes for farmers are all lumped together in the big cauldron that is the never-ending success story of *The Archers*. You can listen in as well, even outside Britain: the BBC has a brilliant internet presence, which offers live streaming and archived material from its radio programmes; TV programmes cannot be viewed outside Her Majesty's realm.

For those of us who have grown up outside Britain, the BBC World Service will have been an important part of our education about the country. The Service, which is funded by the Foreign Office, was set up in 1932. Today, it broadcasts in 28 languages and reaches around 140 million listeners. The World Service played a decisive role during the Second World War, when it broadcast information to the people in occupied Europe. German opponents of the Nazis, such as the winner of the Nobel Prize for Literature, Thomas Mann, and many others, used the German service to broadcast their views; Charles de Gaulle kept the French Resistance alive with his speeches. During the Cold War era, the BBC World Service was the preferred source of information behind the Iron Curtain, owing very much to its decidedly non-ideological stance.

The BBC's worldwide reputation rests largely on the work of the World Service, and today the BBC's brand recognition worldwide is up there with the likes of Coca Cola or McDonald's. To own such a brand, based on such a powerful and efficient news gathering and news dissemination machine, should be any nation's dream. But these are the days of efficient management; over the past decade, BBC bureaucrats have closed down around a dozen language programmes and stopped broadcasting to large parts of the world. It may save a bit of money, but, to paraphrase the traditional warning addressed to the popes: *Sic transit vox mundi.*

Melton Mowbray, Leicestershire

*A place to whet your appetite
and leave the table satisfied*

Food, glorious food. Well, when it comes to food we on the continent tend to look at England with a mixture of pity and despair. For us, it is a given that the *Handbook of Fine English Cuisine* must be one of the slimmest books in the world.

My own introduction to English food took place in Lancing, on the day I arrived for a two-week language course. My host family dished up cold ham, cold potatoes, a celery stick, a slice of tomato – and this was the culinary highlight of the fortnight that lay ahead of me.

But Europeans other than those from the blessed Mediterranean countries should hold their breath before lambasting English food. What's so great about pork and cabbage in Germany or Poland? Do dumplings really deserve a Michelin star? Wouldn't the world have survived if 'Jansson's Secret' from Sweden had forever remained a secret? And do we not all recall meals in Italy or France when we were served atrocious, inedible stuff?

Just like the national cuisines of Germany, Scandinavia

or Central Europe, English food is facing the uphill struggle against the dominant Mediterranean cuisines: if you do not have the aromas of the south, you have to be very good to compete. 'The best English cooking is of course, French cooking', or: 'There are two sorts of bad food: Hotel food and English food' – these are just two examples of a wealth of cheap jokes at the expense of English cooking.

For centuries, travellers have remarked on the pitiful state of English cooking, and Voltaire is said to have quipped that the English have 42 religions, but only two sauces. George Orwell complained in his essay 'In Defence of English Cooking' that even in England, people were dismissive of their own cooking. He listed English specialities that do not need to fear comparison to any other food in the world, such as Kippers, Yorkshire Pudding, Devonshire Cream, the wonderful cakes and biscuits and of course, the splendid jams and marmalades.

Orwell was right, and there are so many other things that are just fantastic: the good old roast beef is hard to beat; Steak & Kidney Pie may not be the acme of culinary achievement, but properly done, it is a feast! And there is of course, the 'Full English Breakfast', the *shah-of-shahs*, the emperor of all breakfasts. Somerset Maugham famously remarked: 'To eat well in England you should have breakfast three times a day.' And no, this is not to belittle other food.

In recent years there has been an English food renaissance, ironically led by the French chef Raymond Blanc and French-trained English chefs. England has become a wine-drinking nation, in fact, with some 1.6 billion bottles imported to the kingdom every year, it is the world's largest wine importer. And even the humble pork pie from Melton Mowbray, the small Leicestershire town that serves as our stopover for this chapter, has made its mark: it became the first English dish to be given regional trademark protection, just like Parma Ham, Cognac and Champagne.

You can of course buy pork pies wherever you go in England, but there are some distinctions which set the Melton Mowbray pork pie apart from its kin. The most important difference is the meat. While other pork pies are made with minced, cured meat to achieve a smooth texture and pink colour, the Melton Mowbray uses chopped, uncured meat, which means that a true Melton Mowbray pork pie will always be grey and have a rough, chewy texture. It's the perfect nutrition on a hiking trip, and it makes a hearty lunch, with a bit of cheese, salad and mixed pickles.

No army has been able to invade the British Isles since the Normans came over, but French chefs did manage a peaceful invasion, without even blunting their knives. The Victorians may have a reputation for shunning culinary delights but they eagerly employed French chefs. Auguste Escoffier, the 'chef of kings and king of chefs' spent much of the time between 1890 and 1920 working in London, becoming the yardstick against which all others' efforts were measured.

It is not easy to say what makes food English food. The influences from the continent and of course, from the food brought by immigrants are tremendous. Fish & Chips, which we all learn at school to be the archetypal English fast food, has lost ground and plays third fiddle (at best) to Chinese take-aways and Indian curries. These are the most consumed foods in England, possibly because they are so addictive: it has been scientifically proven that the spices contained in curries increase blood pressure and heart rate and create the wish to repeat the experience, with hotter spices, please.

Historically, there are many reports of the splendid feasts the English dished up for their foreign visitors. Cartoons such as Hogarth's *The Gates of Calais* contrasted the ruddy-cheeked English beef eaters with their famished counterparts across the channel. One often hears that the Victorians ended this great tradition. But why would they have done that? If you look at cook books published in the nineteenth century, there is no hint at a sudden turn to the frugal. Take the example of 'Tabitha Tickletooth', the pseudonym used by the actor Charles Selby, who published *The Dinner Question; Or: How to Dine Well & Economically* in 1860: it is full of delicious recipes and advice on how to manage a household, hygiene and an overview of London restaurants. The legendary cook book by Mrs. Beeton, written around the same time, influenced English cooking well into the twentieth century.

The demise of English cooking came with the Second World War, when rationing had to be introduced. The United Kingdom had been dependent on food imports for almost two centuries by then, and the German blockade meant that severe measures had to be taken. From January 1940, everything except bread, potatoes and Fish & Chips was rationed. Rationing was even extended to bread and potatoes after the war had ended; this sorry state of affairs lasted until 1954.

Fourteen years of rationing turned the country into a culinary desert. Take cheese as an example: before the war, there were small cheese makers dotted all over the country. These were all closed down and all milk had to be delivered to large industrial dairies. By law, these were required to produce only two sorts of cheese: Cheddar for the masses, and Stilton for the ladies and gentlemen to have with port and walnuts after a good dinner. Only in the past twenty years has there been a re-emergence of small scale cheese making, and these cheeses are some of the best in the world, in terms of taste and craftsmanship.

The food served up for lunch in schools may also have contributed to the downturn in English culinary tastes. For decades it has been an easy target for governments trying to reduce spending. Margaret Thatcher was especially helpful during her years as Education Secretary: she scrapped the free distribution of milk to schoolchildren, which earned her the nickname 'Maggie Thatcher, Milk Snatcher'. Her reasoning may have had to do with the fact that since time untold, public schools had been run along the golden principle that the more they charged in fees, the more atrocious the food they served up. It's all part of the pedagogic principle: if you survive public school food, you will survive anything; you can manage with a 'stiff upper lip', even though it may make it a bit difficult to eat your soup without splashing.

The French influence on today's English cooking goes to the very foundation of food philosophy: take good local produce, handle them with respect and let your imagination fly. Today, it is quite safe to take part in one of the many local food festivals and you may be able to treat yourself to delights you would not find anywhere outside England. York uses its food festival to celebrate York as a *terroir* in the French sense – possibly one of the few examples where state-sponsored *terroirism* is welcome.

This renewed awareness has translated itself into an onslaught of cooking programmes on TV and a plethora of cook books (big type, big pictures, lots of white spaces) in the bestseller lists. Celebrity chefs such as Jamie Oliver, Marco Pierre White, Heston Blumenthal or Gordon Ramsay are treated like royalty; Delia Smith's *How to Cook*, which explains the very basics of preparing food, was a bestseller even in France! The untold hours of TV cooking has certainly improved the *décor* of kitchens – the must-have item for the better off is an 'Aga'; it is a monstrous thing that has to be kept running 24 hours a day and cooks, bakes, fries and boils water all at once. It weighs probably as much as a wrecked ocean liner, costs a bomb and emits something like six tons of CO_2 per year.

But you cannot eat an oven, and TV has not really improved the standards of English home cooking. Most people will enjoy watching the 'domestic goddess' Nigella Lawson (*Nigella* is Latin for cumin; but she's named after her father Nigel, the former Chancellor) preparing delicious food, and then pop something into the microwave – just as many people on the continent will do. And, just as on the continent, too many people pay too little respect to the animal which has given its life to be prepared for dinner.

Basic cooking skills are a dying art form, which is why Jamie Oliver's ambitious programmes to teach these skills in local academies and to bring decent food to school canteens have been so important. The results are not over-impressive: when Oliver's meals were served up in schools, the children hated it. If you have never tasted a fresh salad in your life, how are you supposed to react? Droves of mothers lined up at school perimeter walls to hand over Mars bars, burgers and other fare which they perceived as healthy – after all, you need your daily overdose of sugar and fat to grow up to proper obesity, don't you? Oliver has kept up his fight for almost a decade, and never hesitates to take on the Powers That Be in his quest for better food. I am not overly impressed by his cook books – but for this effort, he deserves my highest respect.

When I say that English food has become much better, I certainly won't deny that there are still dreadful things around: Mother's Pride bread would bring tears to any proud mother's eyes on the continent; Marmite or potato crisps with outland-ish flavours such as 'Cajun Squirrel' (yes, I have seen it), and possibly 'Footballer's Socks' (no, I made that one up); as for the 'bangers', the cheap sausages you are likely to get for breakfast, well, they have been the target of jokes for decades. Whether they are real food is up for debate, and I pity the poor animals who have given their meat for such an undeserving end.

So, you should be aware that even today you may be treated to abysmal fare in England; but you are also very likely to find surprisingly good food. It will cost you a bundle, but when it comes to Michelin stars, London is second only to Paris. So dig in, but make sure your credit line is intact.

Milton Keynes, Buckinghamshire

A place to Do It Oneself;
of spillovers and expensive ladders

Dear reader, my suggestion to stop over in Milton Keynes during our tour of England may come as a surprise to you. 'But there's nothing there!' you will say, and you are almost correct. But just because a town isn't much to look at does not mean that it is not interesting. And Milton Keynes is interesting. Not just because it is home to some of the worst modernist municipal architecture you may clap eyes on anywhere in the kingdom. The fact that it is also home to MK Dons FC, which proudly bestrode the higher divisions of English football when it was still based in Wimbledon, is also not such an attraction. Milton Keynes is interesting because it is part of the last wave of 'new towns' that were built in the 1960s and 1970s, designed to cope with the overspill of population of nearby urban centres and to ease the pressure on the housing market.

Situated some 50 miles north-west of London, Milton Keynes is ideally located to serve the metropolitan areas around London, in the Midlands and even in the Greater Manchester area. Train connections are good, housing is reasonably priced and the civic infrastructure does not leave too many things to be desired. Except, probably, for the feeling of a town that has some sort of cohesion; Milton Keynes may have parks and trees and good shopping centres, but the radically employed grid system also means that there is no sense of togetherness. However, my friend Alistair, who has been living there for more than 30 years, likes it. So, who am I to judge?

The New Town movement is an interesting phenomenon when it comes to the history of housing in England. Following the industrial boom era in the nineteenth century, all the industrial centres became hugely overpopulated, affording only the basest living conditions to the urban poor. During the second part of the nineteenth century, some efforts were made to address the problem of overpopulation; around the mill towns, factories and collieries, model settlements were created to house workers and their families. But a proper solution came only when overspill settlements were created around the industrial centres in the twentieth century. Garden cities such as Letchworth, founded in 1903, or Welwyn Garden City in the 1920s, led the way, but it was only after the Second World War that more than a dozen new towns were created in a structured effort. Even today, despite there being no more government agencies to oversee the creation of new towns, settlements are being planned to offer more affordable housing in sometimes pastoral surroundings – Prince Charles's effort at Poundbury in Dorset is just one of these.

The new town movement shows the enormous importance

housing has to the English – much more so than on the continent. We foreigners like to grin at sayings such as 'My Home is My Castle' or 'Home, Sweet Home', which you could see embroidered on cushion covers whenever you were invited to an English family's home. It may well be that the English enthusiasm for their private homes derives from the fact most of them actually own their homes (or at least pay a mortgage for it). Almost 80 per cent of the apartments and houses in England are owned by their occupiers; that is about twice the rate of ownership you find in countries such as Germany or Italy.

A proper Englishman grows up with the firm belief that to own his living quarters is the ultimate goal in life. Building society accounts (when building societies were still around) were often opened for you right after you were born, and it is still quite customary for people in their twenties to purchase their first flat or house. This first dwelling will be sold off after a couple of years to finance the acquisition of a new space. It is not uncommon for people to buy and sell four or five properties during their life; the system is called the 'housing ladder' – on the continent, most people stick to the one purchase they made for life.

This belief in real estate is partly grounded in sensible thinking: why would you want to pay rent when the same amount of money can buy you a property over the years? The common psyche may also remember the times before the First World War, when only those who owned their houses were allowed to vote. No politician can afford to criticise this belief, even though the recently burst real estate bubble clearly exposed the perils that come with it. Sure, the situation Engels described in the slums of London or Manchester does not exist as drastically in today's England. But for anyone who cannot afford to buy, finding a place to live is extremely difficult. If you are really poor, local councils are obliged to provide you with low-rental housing; but if you earn even slightly more than what defines the poverty line, you are between a rock and a hard place. Year after year, district councils and the government come up with proposals to build affordable housing for 'key workers' such as nurses, teachers or policemen; the effects of these policies are negligible.

For those who have managed to get their foot on the property ladder, this situation is totally different. In the metropolitan areas, property prices keep on rising and have even weathered the brief downturn after the property bubble burst; over the past twenty years, annual increases of 10 or even 15 per cent in a property's value have come to be seen as perfectly normal in most parts of London – at the same time, the government poured millions into the destruction of dilapidated housing estates in the former industrial centres in the north.

Most private properties are one-family homes; only 30 per cent of the dwellings constructed each year are flats.* This may

---

* Ministry for Communities and Local Government: *House Building: December Quarter 2011, England.*

have to do with the English yearning for privacy; most back gardens are fenced in a way that doesn't allow even a glimpse inside. This is where the Englishman's home becomes his castle, and with moats and walls not being very practical in a suburban setting, one has to make do with a bit of wood and a tall hedge. Renovating and decorating these castles of our day is a special English pastime; walls get clad with fake Tudor beams, perfectly working windows are replaced with crown glass and you may also find Doric columns in front of humble terraced houses.

All these delightful atrocities are possible because the English tend to be ardent followers of the cult of Do-It-Yourself. Across the nation, some £16 billion is spent each year in DIY shops and garden centres. In other countries, Easter may be the celebration of the crucifixion and resurrection of Christ; in England, it is the official start of the DIY season. More than three times as many people as on normal weekends visit DIY shops, and the A & E units of the hospitals are in true emergency mode as they treat the wounds sustained in the pursuit of the noble cause, with shelving units attached to knees, saw blades embedded in arms and bodies used to test whether the electricity has really been cut off.

Given this readiness to sacrifice life and limb for the sprucing up of one's home, we should not be surprised to find that the most successful bits of daytime TV are of course shows about interior design and property development. *Homes under the Hammer*, which shows how houses bought at auction can be transformed, has been a hit for years; and series such as *Changing Rooms* in which neighbours or friends were let loose to redecorate each other's homes may have caused more bloodshed and tears than every slasher movie ever shown.

The Moon under Water

Wherever I pay my tab, that's my home

'No, Sir; there is nothing which has yet been contrived by man, by which so much happiness is produced as by a good tavern or inn.'

(James Boswell, *Life of Johnson*)

Apart from the Royals, no other English institution is held in higher esteem than the traditional English pub. We have our cafés on the continent, our beer gardens and bistros – but the pub is a different thing; a good 'local' is an extension of one's private sphere, a home from home that occupies the sensitive place between the public and the private. Once you have found your 'local', you stick with it; there are no faults. You may have noticed already that George Orwell is one of my favourite observers of English life, and even though most of his writings are now some 70 years old, his observations ring true even today. In his 1946 essay, 'The Moon Under Water', he describes his ideal pub; it is a Victorian boozer fair and square, with frosted glass and private nooks and hearty pub snacks, good beer and, most importantly, no disturbing noise emanating from radios or music piped into the room that drowns out conversation. I could not agree more, especially with his insistence that a pub is no place for music to be played out loud.

As I said, we foreigners love English pubs, but in the past, we always found one major fly in the ointment: the visiting hours, especially before Maggie Thatcher relaxed them. Why would one close a decent place of entertainment and refuge from the perils of the world outside during the afternoon? Why kick out your customers just as they have begun to settle in properly? We never understood.

During the First World War, closing times were introduced to prevent workers from taking alcoholic refreshments during their breaks. After the war, prohibitionist activism made sure the pubs stayed shut between 1:30 p.m. and 6 p.m. Brewers and publicans did not mind too much: overall consumption did not go down; it was just crammed into a shorter time. Working shorter hours and still making the same amount of money was just fine by the people in the industry.

Well, the rigid closing times are a thing of the past, thanks in part to the arguments put forth by the police forces who found controlling masses of drunken people who popped out into the streets all at the same time slightly stressful. Many pubs still tend to throw out their customers at 11 p.m. sharp, but there are quite a lot around these days who will let you drink in peace and quiet until a later hour. Misgivings that these relaxed opening times might lead to the country drowning in a large ocean of beer were misplaced, overall consumption has not risen sharply. And when we compare alcohol consumption in Europe, the English are not so bad. According to the World Health Organisation they consume 13.4 litres of alcohol a year, slightly less than the French with 13.7 litres. Europe's top boozers are the Moldovans who manage to force 18.2 litres down their throats.*

Today, pubs are places not only for male drinkers, but also for families. They have been re-established as places to eat, a tradition that had all but disappeared after the Second World War, and there are even some pubs which have been awarded Michelin stars and other gourmet ratings. In rural areas, some pubs double up as post offices or local shops, providing much needed community services.

Pubs have been part of English life for centuries – even though the name has been around only since Victorian times. Before that, they were simply 'taverns', a name derived from the Roman *tabernae* which actually were the first public drinking places on the island. The role of these drinking places increased through the times, especially with the expansion of national and international trade, which called for places where travellers could rest and merchants could meet. Many of these early 'inns' were run by monks who also established the first

---

* Global status report on Alcohol and Health. Geneva, 2011.

large-scale brewing operations; some of these places are still in operation today.

Alehouses, which catered for the lower classes, and taverns, which served wine and were much more expensive, co-existed happily throughout the centuries, and the image of the cosy tavern with its open fireplace and content, well-fed gentlemen drinkers has survived well into our days.

When I got to know the pleasures of the English pubs, at the end of the 1970s, drinking habits had been changing. Out went the sturdy, traditional ales and milds and bitters, in came tasteless industrial fizzy drinks with a sickly yellow colour. The English called them lager and thought they were now drinking cool continental beers. As a German, I know my 'Pils' and in those days we would not have touched the stuff that the English were fobbed off with. More's the pity, because a proper English ale or bitter is right up there with the tastiest types of beer imaginable. Fortunately, the 'Campaign for Real Ale' (CAMRA) has battled relentlessly to save the traditional beers, and with great success. No self-respecting pub today would be content to serve only one type of ale, quite often you will find a selection; some pub chains even reach out to local breweries and feature 'guest beers', for the benefit of the customers and pub culture in general.

Pubs may be one of the most important ingredients of English popular culture, but this does not mean that they are not endangered: thanks to the huge valuations of property, investment companies formed huge conglomerates during the 1990s; some of these highly leveraged 'pubcos' had up to 9,000 pubs under management. When the property crisis hit in 2008, their business models collapsed like a world class drinker at the taste of mineral water. Towards the end of the first decade of the twenty-first century, around 40 pubs per week went out of business. That's what I call a crisis!

Blackpool, Lancashire

Where we are reminded of fools and Englishmen
and meet a travelling Cook

Oh, the pleasures of Blackpool! Golden sands on the beaches, cold beer in the glass, and Fish & Chips on the table. Could you wish for a better place to go on a holiday?

Well actually, yes, you can – that's what the English tend to say these days. Patronage of the holiday resorts around England's coasts has drastically bottomed out since cut-price air travel came to the island and evacuated the work-weary masses to more pleasant – and much more reliably sunny – places.

But it all somehow started with Blackpool, thanks to the eighteenth century fad of bathing in the sea; the salt water was supposed to cure diseases. A stage coach service to Blackpool was established in the 1780s, a couple of hotels and entertainment facilities followed suit. The real boom started in 1846, when a railway link was established, meaning the aspiring middle classes from the prosperous northern towns and cities could make the trip without too much effort. Blackpool grew rapidly on the basis of a continuous stream of visitors who marveled at ever-expanding establishments, such as three separate entertainment piers, music halls and the famous Winter

Garden, which boasted the Opera House, the largest outside of London. It even became the world's first town to have electrical street lighting. In its heyday in the 1950s, Blackpool received some 17 million visitors per year, making it one of Europe's most popular holiday destinations.

The concept of travelling for leisure first took root in England in the eighteenth century. Of course, for most people even a trip to the next town remained an exciting feat, but the wealthier layers of society indulged in the new pastime with ardent rigour. The 'Grand Tour' was born, and every young Englishman of class just had to traipse around Europe to visit the ancient sites in Greece and Italy, travel to the Alps or along the Rhine. The entire European tourist industry was started by this English fashion, and it was no coincidence that an Englishman was the first commercially successful tourism entrepreneur: Thomas Cook.

Cook, who was a Baptist preacher, was an active campaigner for the temperance movement and in 1841, he arranged for a party of 540 people to travel together from Leicester to Loughborough to attend a temperance rally. The trip may have only been eleven miles, but it changed the world. Cook found that he could earn money by arranging tours, and he started offering excursions at cheap prices on a regular basis. It was a roaring success; the railways loved him for the business he provided; the people cherished the opportunity to leave their none-too-pleasant urban surroundings for a short while; Cook loved the income he generated for himself and his family.

Starting with that eleven mile excursion, there was no looking back: trips to Europe, America, the Middle East and even around the world – over the years, with improving transport links, Cook's company made it possible for millions of people to go to places they were hitherto only able to dream about. Cook even introduced an early version of the Traveller's Cheque.

Resorts like Blackpool sprung up all around the British Isles; the annual trip became a middle class luxury that one simply could not do without. Simple pleasures were called for: amusement arcades and pubs; deckchairs and smutty postcards to send home. The English coastal resorts provided all this and thrived, at least until the 1970s, when the general downturn in the economy and the reluctance on the resorts' part to adapt to the times brought about a lamentable decline in fortunes. As I said before, most English holiday-makers prefer destinations abroad, and when you go to the old coastal resorts you will find fine examples of decay. Hotels and other accommodation stand empty for months; many of them exude the charm of a bygone era and the stale air of decades of deferred maintenance works. If you are a fan of black-and-white photography, these are the places you should go to.

Savile Row, London

A street fit to fit the gentleman

There are not many industries or crafts in which England has been able to maintain a leading position. Exclusive men's wear is one of them, and it doesn't get much more exclusive than Savile Row in London's Mayfair, where most mortals would probably need to take out a second mortgage on their home to be able to afford a bespoke suit. The area was developed in the 1730s and soon became home to many tailors; since the nineteenth century, the top end of the industry has been concentrated here. Although not too many businesses have survived the onslaught of more relaxed standards in business dress on the one hand and sky-rocketing property prices on the other, Savile Row and the streets adjacent to it have remained a Mecca for an international clientele of discerning gentlemen with appropriate lines of credit.

It is not only the craftsmanship of English tailors which sets them apart from their colleagues on the continent (except for Italy); it is the particular style of the well-made English suit and the allure of the ideal of the gentleman, that has gripped the world's imagination. The English suit has a shorter and slimmer jacket than its continental counterpart; the trousers reach higher, they are also leaner and do not have turn-ups. A business suit has to be either dark blue, charcoal grey or black; patterns such as pinstripe or nailhead are acceptable. Obviously, fashion has nothing to do with it; in 2009, *Esquire* magazine named Prince Charles the world's Best Dressed Man, and Charles's dress sense is as staunchly conservative as could be imagined. His double-breasted suits have been out of fashion for decades, as have his ties and shirts. But the overall impression is extremely stylish, possibly exactly because of its decisive avoidance of fashion trends.

Conservatism explains most of the English dress sense – many employers require male employees to wear a suit and tie to work and some even used to discourage female staff from wearing trousers in the office; formal dress is called for on numerous occasions and most schools have no room for jeans and t-shirts when it comes to prescribing school uniforms. Some years ago, a girl had to fight her way up to the High Court to be allowed to forego the mandatory skirt that was part of her school's uniform. All these rules and formality, alas, do not mean that the English have a better dress sense than the rest of us. Quite the contrary is true: there is hardly another country in Europe where you can see so many cheap and ill-fitting suits and costumes.

Apart from the Savile Row suit, English men's wear has given the world quite a number of iconic garments: the tweed sports jacket and the blazer, corduroy trousers, wax jackets, trench and duffel coats. They are all practical, sensible and slightly dull. English ladies' wear has never produced such icons, even the 'House Check' you find in all clothes sold under the Burberry brand was originally designed for men's wear.

In most foreigners' minds, the most English of all things you can wear is still the bowler hat. Sadly, the bowler hat is quite unfashionable these days and you won't see too many of them being worn outside racecourses or market halls. They have been around since 1849, when the Earl of Leicester became annoyed with the high cost of repairs for the top hats his game keepers wore. Riding through the nobleman's forests, these top hats were frequently knocked off their wearers' heads; a new and sturdy article of head gear had to be found. The Earl's younger brother was dispatched to London to confer with leading hat makers, and the firm of James Lock came up with the winning design. The sturdiness was achieved by adding shellac to the felt. Rumour has it that the client tested the prototype by repeatedly jumping on it. The first batches of hats were produced by the contracting hatmakers Bowler Brothers, and this is where the name comes from.

The bowler was an immediate success throughout the country and across class boundaries. It was practical and useful and was worn on any occasion by anybody – the first truly classless garment. The humble bowler even attracted a number of aliases: in the north, it is still sometimes referred to as the 'billycock'; and because you could see so many of them at racecourses, the name 'derby' became popular, as well.

If you need a stylish souvenir from your trip to England, you may wish to try a bowler hat; James Lock & Co has provided its customers with hats since 1676 – its shop in St. James's Street is well worth a visit.

St. Austell, Cornwall

We go here and hope to live another day,
along with the shrubs

The English love their parks and gardens, and the annual summer drought (yes, we are still in England) always provides ample material for TV and tabloids, when nice old ladies and tough old duffers tell the woeful stories about how their gherkins and carrots and parsnips have come a cropper, again. On the continent, we may shrug at such stories, but this is because we lack the understanding that whilst the English may be a great seafaring nation, deep down in their hearts, they have always been gardeners.

The private plot or back garden may be the crowning glory of many English people's existence but the phenomenal public parks and gardens are certainly the crowning glory of England as a nation. Kew Gardens and Hyde Park, Blenheim, Sissinghurst and so many others offer such pleasure to the eye and mind that one easily forgives the follies and foibles of English politics and everyday life. Most of the great parks date back to the eighteenth and nineteenth centuries, but the most ambitious project of them all came to life only in 2001: the Eden Project in St. Austell, just a couple of miles into Cornwall.

Here we find two massive conservatories, along with a huge open park space. More than 100,000 plants from all over the world are on display. The first 'biome' is the world's largest conservatory; it would be big enough to hold the entire Tower of London. It simulates tropical conditions with high humidity; the climate in the second biome resembles the Mediterranean. Outside, there are plants from temperate areas, as you would expect. You may have seen these amazing structures if you have seen the James Bond movie, *Die Another Day*.

The whole project is designed not only as a showcase for the world's vegetation, but also as a reminder of the fragility of our ecosystems. This may sound frightfully didactic, and it certainly aims to teach people something but I cannot find fault with that – after all, even if you do not attend lectures and guided tours, you are guaranteed to have a jolly good time in these amazing surroundings. More than a million visitors come here every year, despite the fact that St. Austell is rather far away from almost anywhere in England.

As one can imagine, gardening plays a huge role in the public psyche. Everything that is connected to gardening attracts huge interest; the annual 'Chelsea Flower Show' is one of the most important events in the social diary. Even Prince Charles regularly exhibits here. Two thirds of the English population claim to be active gardeners, and this has been reflected for years in the media schedules. *Gardener's Question Time* has been a Sunday afternoon staple on BBC Radio 4 for decades, giving proper (if slightly boring) advice about what to do with your potatoes, squash or begonias. *Ground Force* on TV has taken the opposite approach, a kind of flower-power version of the Cinderella story: a neglected patch gets transformed into a botanic treasure trove, seemingly in no time. The protagonists of the programme have all become bestselling authors and veritable sex symbols – well, some aspects of the English psyche are probably better left untouched.

I said before that the private garden is something like the crowning glory of a person's existence, and it often is; the front garden, which is cruelly exposed to the glances of everybody, is normally kept in good nick in order to impress the neighbours and underline your bourgeois credentials. Flower beds, little water features and the ubiquitous garden gnome are staples of these presentations, which would certainly please General Potemkin. But you will hardly ever see the owner here, apart from the times when he or she trims and primps the plants.

The back garden is another matter entirely. The little plot of land behind your house, lovingly protected from prying eyes, serves the English need for privacy perfectly. And this also means that people tend to ease off the rigid standards they apply to the space in front of the house. You may well find heaps of grass cut years ago, and more often than one might think, the biggest part of the garden may be paved. This is where the English are at their most relaxed – and relaxation does not always go well with arduous work.

Royal Albert Hall, London

Where Britannia rules and God saves the Queen;
and ferries crossing the Mersey are important too

One of the most beloved seasons in the English music lover's year is 'Prom Season' in the summer, when 'The Henry Wood Promenade Concerts presented by the BBC' put on 100 classical concerts in London and many other places across the country. Founded in 1895, the series is the world's largest music festival and its attraction has spread around the globe. Tickets are benevolently priced, and the atmosphere throughout the individual events is one of leisure and enjoyment. Many concerts take place in parks, as one would expect from a 'promenade' season, but the Royal Albert Hall remains the centre of the programme. The final concert evening, the 'Last Night of the Proms' has become a global television event; the audience tends to sport some kind of fancy dress and the boisterous mood of camaraderie, flag-waving and light-hearted, ironic jingoism (especially during the final sequence which always includes staples such as 'Rule Britannia' and 'Jerusalem') projects an image of England as a nation that really knows how to enjoy itself. You may well be in with a chance of getting a ticket, although the process is a bit convoluted.

The Royal Albert Hall, which was opened in 1871, was originally designed as a multi-purpose hall, to be used especially for exhibitions. Over time, it became London's premier spot for musical events, even though the acoustics were never up to scratch for top performances. But, as with so many things in England, these deficiencies do not really matter; one comes here because it is a thing one simply does.

As to the music at the Proms, most of it is part of the tried and tested classical canon: Mozart, Strauss, Verdi and the other great Europeans feature heavily; English composers do not get too much attention. This is with good reason: English classical composers are simply a bit second rate. The most important of them was the German import, Georg Friedrich Händel, who had come to England in 1710 and became a successful music entrepreneur – his 'Zadok the Priest' is still the music of choice during coronation ceremonies. England continued to import great composers, conductors and performers from the continent; in the nineteenth century, Felix Mendelssohn became a strong influence on English composers, visiting frequently and even mentoring promising musicians who were invited to his conservatory in Leipzig; Wagner and Grieg were also held as musical heroes. The founding of professional orchestras propelled the English musical scene into a new era, with the Royal Philharmonic Orchestra in Liverpool leading the way from 1840; the Hallé in Manchester and the Royal Opera in London's Covent Garden followed suit.

Gustav Holst, Ralph Vaughan Williams and Edward Elgar

came out of this musical tradition. Elgar's music in particular, including the 'Enigma Variations' and his 'Pomp and Circumstance', dominate the second part of the Last Night of the Proms. These pieces proved to be highly popular fare, and they are certainly that: popular, entertaining and very mainstream. Elgar himself was an interesting man: a one-time bandmaster at the Worcester lunatic asylum, he opened Abbey Road studios, which were later made famous by The Beatles, and even composed a hymn for his beloved Wolverhampton Wanderers FC.

Holst, Vaughan Williams and Elgar all came to prominence around the turn of the century. Never denying continental influences, they developed a musical style which can be seen as distinctly English. Whilst on the continent, the harmonic system was being challenged, English composers continued very much in that tradition. A generation later, Benjamin Britten was able to distance himself from this tradition, which he perceived as insular. His own highly original musical tone established him as one of the world's leading classical composers of the twentieth century.

So, when it comes to classical music, England has not had much to offer that would be of interest musically and historically. But when it comes to pop music, England leads the world. Today, pop music is one of the country's most important export products, thanks to a tradition established in the 1960s with the Mersey Beat of bands like The Beatles and Gerry and the Pacemakers, or the offerings of today's most successful band of OAPs – The Rolling Stones. Then, the younger generation lapped up the new music to distinguish themselves from their parents, establishing a genuine youth culture, which was not born in the marketing departments of the music and fashion industries.

Beat took hold in 1960s Liverpool and spread throughout the country when the big dance halls were closed to Rock 'n' Roll – if one wanted to hear it, one had to go to small clubs or church halls, where local bands played for little money. Most bands had a limited repertoire, which meant that the organisers would hire more than one band per evening, which in turn created more gigs for each band, who would regularly play two or three venues per night. Even though the fees were small, forming a band became an attractive proposition, and you can hardly spend an evening in a pub anywhere in the north without some old geezer telling you the story of how he just missed out on becoming a star.

In my opinion, the next big step in pop culture came in the late 60s and early 70s, when Punk arrived from the USA. Artists such as Patti Smith or the Ramones had created a loud-mouthed alternative to hippie culture – where flower power saw the world through rose-tinted glasses, Punk rejected all that. England's youth loved it; ten years after The Beatles and Stones, here was a new kind of music that defined the young generation's utter contempt for the status quo. Beat and Rock 'n' Roll had been usurped by the music industry; glam rock and the bombastic, almost symphonic offerings of Yes or Pink

Floyd sugar-coated the original impetus of rock. Bands such as The Clash, The Stranglers or The Sex Pistols provided an alternative and became instant heroes, with their seemingly primitive music and aggressive lyrics. Songs like 'Anarchy in the UK' and 'God Save the Queen' became mega hits. Punk rejected musical virtuosity; one music magazine presented their readers with three basic chords for the guitar: 'Remember them and go start a band!'

As happens with almost every anti-establishment movement, Punk quickly became commercialised. Fashion designers such as Vivienne Westwood created 'Punk Couture' and sold the grungy look at astronomical prices. Punk became a pose. But without it, today's pop music would be very different.

There is, of course, much more to the English pop music scene: Eric Clapton, The Yardbirds, The Who, Pink Floyd and others were, and are, highly influential. There was Ska, which had come to England from the Caribbean and which changed the rhythms and melodies of English pop; rap and hip-hop were massive phenomena. Britpop bands such as Chumbawumba or Oasis were original in their own way. But (and this may be a sign of me getting on a bit) I am no longer all that interested in pop culture – I don't give a toss whether the newest thing is called 'House' or 'Garage' or 'Garden Shed'. Which is okay, I think: pop music is not meant to excite 50-year-olds.

Hoxton, East London

Where the most dangerous sharks don't swim

Hoxton is not what you would call a must-see part of East London; it is poor and generally unkempt, many houses are in desperate need of repair; a dramatic percentage of people depend on benefits. But when it comes to the arts, it really stands out. As in many other cities where poverty-ridden areas have been attractive to students and artists looking for affordable housing and workspaces, Hoxton (as well as nearby Shoreditch, Dalston and Stoke Newington) have been magnets for this community since the 1970s. Gilbert & George paraded the streets as 'living sculpture' and most protagonists of 'Britart' have lived and worked here for a period of time. When the White Cube gallery opened in Hoxton Square in 2000, the status of this dishevelled inner city district as the centre of contemporary art was given quasi-official approval.

The visual arts are not among the traditional strong points of England's culture; in comparison to the great masters from Italy, Germany, Holland or Spain, pre-eighteenth century English painting and sculpture is rather insignificant, and leading talents, such as Hans Holbein the Younger, Van Dyck or Rubens were brought over from the continent to fill the gap. Their work influenced artists like Gainsborough and Reynolds, who led the awakening of visual arts in England. Later, Blake, Constable, Mallard, Turner and others became major influences for the Impressionist movement on the continent, through their innovative way of using light and colour, especially in landscape painting. From the mid-nineteenth century, the decorative arts of the Pre-Raphaelites and the Arts & Crafts movement dominated the scene; this era is best exemplified by the work of William Morris, whose patterns came to be seen as distinctly Victorian.

Following the Second World War, the sculptors Henry Moore and Barbara Hepworth, and painters Lucian Freud, Francis Bacon and David Hockney, made sure that English visual arts stayed up there with the rest of the world. But although these artists may have been influential and commercially successful, it took the 'Young British Artists' (YBAs) to show the world how to milk it.

Both 'YBA' and 'Britart' are catchphrases used to describe a movement that made waves from the late 1980s onwards. Based on the principles of conceptual art, people like Sarah Lucas, Sam Taylor-Wood, Gary Hume and Tracey Emin were propelled into the stratosphere of the art world, thanks to the endorsement of collectors and the art establishment; Damien Hirst even became the world's best-paid artist.

As always when it comes to conceptual art, the YBAs' works have been received controversially. What do you make of Hirst's iconic *The Physical Impossibility of Death in the Mind of Someone Living*? Grand title, great fish: it is a tiger shark preserved in formaldehyde. Hirst had bought the beast from an Australian fisherman in 1991 for £4,000, put it in a glass box and sold it on to Charles Saatchi, the collector who 'made' most of the YBAs, for £50,000. When Saatchi himself had the piece auctioned ten years later, he made a profit of more than £6 million – nice work, if you can get it. By then, the original shark had shrivelled and lost a fin; it has been replaced by a fresh fish now, which obviously has not impaired the value.

When Britart swept onto the scene, it was a breath of fresh air, especially because the movement's protagonists did not wait for grants and subsidies to get on with their work, but understood themselves as commercial artists supplying what was in demand. Hirst et al are true children of the Thatcher era and they were lucky in being able to profit from the pioneering work of artists, such as Gilbert & George or Jeff Koons, who had shocked the art world by using excrement or bodily fluids in their work. Gary Hume nailed a potato to the wall and called it art; Marc Quinn built a sculpture of his head out of five litres of his own frozen blood. Tracey Emin's installation, *My Bed*, which was a bed with dirty linen, a nightstand, paper handkerchiefs, tampons, used condoms and other stuff, was exhibited at the Tate Gallery. When the Chinese performance artists Jian Jun Xi and Yuan Chai used *My Bed* for a public pillow fight, the hip young creator initiated legal proceedings.

Britart has been vehemently criticised by many people who

understand much more about art than I do – personally I feel rather indifferent to it. But the YBAs, who are now in their fifties, have set the stage for a new generation and they have shown how to turn conceptual art into a lucrative business. The new generation work towards an audience which is much more receptive than that of twenty years ago. They may be critical of the YBA forebears; but it only takes a brilliant marketing concept for this young generation to succeed as well.

221b Baker Street, London

Where we light our pipe and settle down to read
some good books and discover verses for monarchs

The address, 221b Baker Street, London, may or may not be the most famous in the world; but it is certainly the address of the world's most famous detective, Sherlock Holmes, and his trusted sidekick, Doctor Watson. When Arthur Conan Doyle wrote the stories about the sleuth, between 1881 and 1904, the address was fictitious – house numbers only ran to 100 at the time. But the demands of the tourist trade called for bricks and mortar, and so today we find the Sherlock Holmes museum at the address; the house is even protected because of its special architectural and historical interest.

All this may sound a little phoney but we are in the realm of literature, after all. And if there is one art form in which the English have always excelled, it is literature. Shakespeare, probably the world's greatest writer, leads the field; Henry Fielding and Joseph Addison, who developed the modern novel in the eighteenth century follow; there are Jane Austen and Lord Byron, Wordsworth, Charles Dickens and so many other writers to read and admire – my love for literature has certainly contributed much to my tender feelings towards England.

With such an august collection of literary greats, you may find it slightly off-hand when I say that the most important contribution England has made to world literature is crime fiction. No other country can boast such a wealth of stylish murders, and so many elegant investigators. Edgar Allen Poe's *Murder in the Rue Morgue* set the ball rolling in 1841. (Poe was born and died in the USA, but he spent much of his youth in the fine London Borough of Stoke Newington, where Daniel Defoe lived before him and I after him.) Poe's stories owed much to the tradition of the Gothic tales which appeared in the late eighteenth century; it was the French author Paul Féval who provided the template for modern crime fiction, with his novel *Jean Diable* which was published in 1862. Féval's hero was Inspector Gregory Temple of Scotland Yard – even though he was a French writer, the setting had to be London.

Why London and England became the setting of so much crime fiction is open to speculation. London, despite being Europe's largest city, was no more crime-ridden than any other big city in those days. Possibly, it was the existence of the new-fangled police, which had been set up by Sir Robert Peel in 1829 (hence the term 'Bobbies') that fascinated writers from all over; since 1842 there had also been a detectives' department, which used new methods to solve crimes.

Arthur Conan Doyle followed in Féval's footsteps some 25 years later with the creation of Sherlock Holmes. The analytical excellence and the reliance on scientific (true or invented) methods set Holmes apart from the other characters that traipsed around the literary world, and established him as the archetype of the English sleuth.

When Sherlock Holmes solved his last case, younger blood had already been drawn by Edgar Wallace, who did not much care for meticulous detection and analysis but spruced up his plots with racy action and suspense. It worked well and by the 1920s, a quarter of all books bought in Britain were by Wallace. He also tried his hand at new media: Wallace wrote the script for the original *King Kong* movie. Francis Durbridge (another great of the English crime writing scene) wrote the long-running radio series *Send for Paul Temple* about the brilliant amateur sleuth (and professional crime writer) Paul Temple. The hero is a treasure of broadcasting history – you can still catch some of the original episodes through the BBC's online service.

Arthur Conan Doyle and Edgar Wallace may have been the kings of the genre, but they were more than matched by the murderous queens of crime: Agatha Christie, with her stories about Miss Marple and Hercule Poirot leads the majestic procession, followed by Dorothy L. Sayers and of course, Ruth Rendell and P.D. James.

Crime fiction has been a mainstay of the publishing industry for many decades. And when it comes to the publishing industry, England leads the world. No other country in the western world produces so many titles per year, and some of its writers rank among the highest-selling authors in the world, with J.K. Rowling and her *Harry Potter* series leading the pack.

Rowling and writers of her ilk are of course, highly commercial and the publishing industry relies heavily on the productivity of these tried and tested producers of writing with a mass appeal. One is not too picky as to the quality of writing: Jamie Oliver's cook books may leave much to be desired in terms of craft; Jeremy Clarkson droning on about his life inside and outside cars might be called mind-numbingly dull; and what do we make of the literary prowess of silicon-enhanced talents such as Katie 'Jordan' Price, who has produced more than 30 books, most of them wild commercial successes?

Enter Alexander Pope, who wrote in his *Dunciad*:

> Thy hand, great Anarch! lets the curtain fall,
> And universal darkness buries all.

England is still a nation of readers and book lovers, but the writing is on the wall. Since 2005, almost half of the bookshops across the country have had to close down. The brutal cuts to civic spending, which came with the budgets of the Conservative-Lib Dem government, have led to the closure of many public libraries; full-time librarians facing redundancy were told they would be welcome to return to their jobs on a voluntary basis as part of the Big Society programme.

But even today, when we tend to think that the publishing industry's crude commercialism has eroded the more refined types of writing, the English love for language and words is very much alive. There are still things such as the weekly *Poetry*

Please programme on Radio 4, which simply broadcasts the poems readers have written in to hear. Transport for London has promoted poetry since 1986 through its 'Poems on the Underground' series – six poems per year are advertised on posters and hoardings in some 3,000 carriages. All very simple, very touching. And poetry even sells, at least in some cases. Ted Hughes, who died in 1998, and Seamus Heaney are the most successful poets – a couple of years ago, an analysis by the Arts Council showed that these two stood for about half of all poetry sales. Other poets receive a steady income from being included in the national curriculum. And every year, there are dozens of competitions for aspiring poets as well as themed anthologies, such as *The Nations Favourite Poems* about love, peace, youth, old age and many other topics.

And there are things which would not be feasible in other countries: Alain de Botton's stint as writer-in-residence at Heathrow Airport is such an example; Barnsley FC, some supermarket chains, the Wimbledon tennis tournament or the rail company Northern Spirit have all at some time employed the services of writers, obviously as a marketing stint, but also because there is a genuine interest in the written and spoken word.

Towering above all these writers-in-residence is the kingdom's Poet Laureate, an office which was introduced in 1668. The main job of the Poet Laureate is to write amiable verses upon special occasions – royal weddings, funerals, birthdays, jubilees, visits to foreign lands and such things. Not every one of the 22 gentlemen (the present incumbent, Carol Ann Duffy, is the first woman to have been chosen) who have held the post can be said to have contributed timeless prose or poetry; in fact, quite a lot of them were of a rather mediocre calibre. Maybe the lousy pay was to blame – traditionally, they received one cask of sherry per year, for life. Only since Andrew Motion took on the post in 1999 has there been an annual remuneration of £5,000.

John Dryden, the first Laureate, was a towering giant among his colleagues and it certainly helped that he tended to pen poems which were favourable to the governing Whig party. But good poets are not necessarily good diplomats, and Dryden blotted his copybook by converting to Catholicism and refusing to follow King William III; thus, the first Laureate to be appointed was also the first one to be fired. His successor, Thomas Shadwell, was more of a poetic garden gnome but his humble offerings pleased the none-too-developed tastes of the royal couple. Shadwell set the tone for a tradition of laureates and laureates' writing that make one shudder today. Nahum Tate, Shadwell's successor, is best remembered for writing a happy ending to Shakespeare's *King Lear*. Laurence Eusden, who came to the office in 1775, still crops up today with wonderful examples of rhymed stupidity, with gems such as 'Thy virtues shine particularly nice / Ungloomed with a confinity to vice' – well, if George III was not already off his rocker at the time, such writing may well have contributed to his deteriorating condition. By the nineteenth century,

Sir Walter Scott – who had rejected the post – called for an end to this particular form of public cruelty. But where in the world would a monarch or a government part with the noble tradition of poetic sycophancy?

From the mid-1800s, things improved: Hazlitt, Wordsworth and Tennyson took the job, and they were all superb poets. Wordsworth even refused to write a single praise poem during his tenure, and Tennyson ignored quite a lot of the royal occasions during his 40 years in office. But of course, this unpatriotic silence had to come to an end, and Alfred Austin, the ultra-conservative leader writer of the *Daily Express* took it upon himself to restore the office's former glory. When Queen Victoria's son fell ill, he rhymed: 'Across the wires the electric message came / he is not better; he is much the same.' And a fateful battle during the Boer War led him to the eternally beautiful: 'They went across the veldt / As hard as they could pelt'. Old age caused him to get even more of his wires crossed; he filled a poem commissioned upon a royal visit to Austria with allusions to kangaroos and koala bears – certainly too bizarre even by his own standards. His successors throughout the twentieth century were a disappointment to the collectors of poetic disasters: John Masefield, Cecil Day Lewis, John Betjeman and Ted Hughes simply did not do stupid stuff.

When Ted Hughes died, there were heated discussions as to the relevance of the office of Poet Laureate and of course, about the poets who were thought to be in the running.

Seamus Heaney and Derek Walcott were named as favourites; both had received the Nobel Prize for Literature and would have been excellent choices. But the job went to Andrew Motion, a tried and tested poet of middling repute, teacher of creative writing and ardent supporter of the Labour Party. The 'literati' were not amused and much blood had to be mopped up after the literary critics and rival poets had had their say. Which brings Jonathan Swift to mind, who once wrote:

> What poet would not grieve to see
> His brother write as well as he
> But rather than they should excel
> Would wish his rivals all in Hell?

But Motion, who only agreed upon a ten year tenure, discharged his duties honourably and used his position for the ruthless promotion of poetry in schools and the setting up of the National Poetry Archive. His successor, Carol Ann Duffy, is the most read modern poet in the country, thanks to her work being part of the curriculum. She is also not too active as a praise poet to the royal family – but she did insist that her 600 bottles of sherry be delivered up front.

Goodbye and Thank You

We have come to the end of our little tour around England, and I hope you enjoyed the trip. We have seen a lot of places and heard about many people and events which shaped the country as it is today. I am well aware that I have only been able to touch upon the surface of many things; but I hope that this may motivate you to dig a little deeper wherever I have been able to whet your appetites. There are also many more books on England and the English that are well worth your attention; if my book should get you interested in finding out more about the county and its people, or if it might accompany you for a little while as a trusty companion, then I have achieved what I set out to do.

So, I thank you for your patience and your sympathy.

Thanks are also due to many people who have been helpful. There is the wonderful mother-and-daughter team of Ilse and Barbara Haus Schwepcke who have taken this project on; and Zoë Rutherford, my meticulous editor who managed to pinpoint my mistakes ever so politely and with such great charm. Over the years, friends such as Frank »the Pedant«

Wiedemann, Paul Westlake, Malcolm Imrie, Martina Dervis, Paul Marsh, Tony Mulliken, Geoffrey Davis, John Gardiner, Margaret Ling, Anne Beech, Kate Evans-Jones, Andrew Cousins, Christina Wiedemann, Christoph Links, Edda Fensch and Madjid Semnar have provided assistance and advice and sometimes even wisdom. There is my first English teacher, Heinrich König; my "boss" at Göttingen university, Heinz-Joachim Müllenbrock, who has turned me into a fan of the English landscape garden; colleagues such as Fritz-Wilhelm Neumann and Reinhard Küsgen; my university buddies Annette Hinrichs, Daniel Scheschkewitz, Stefan Anders, Joachim Johannessohn and Thomas Schirmer, who made studying English literature fun.

I will be forever grateful to my father who made it possible for me to visit England. And there is always Monika, who puts up with my follies and ideas.

I bid you all a fond farewell with Puck's words:

> If we shadows have offended,
> Think but this, and all is mended,
> That you have but slumber'd here
> While these visions did appear.
> And this weak and idle theme,
> No more yielding but a dream,
> Gentles, do not reprehend:
> if you pardon, we will mend:

And, as I am an honest Puck,
If we have unearned luck
Now to 'scape the serpent's tongue,
We will make amends ere long;
Else the Puck a liar call;
So, good night unto you all.
Give me your hands, if we be friends,
And Robin shall restore amends.

Farewell, goodbye, and see you soon.

Bibliography

Ackroyd, Peter. *London. The Biography*. London: Vintage, 2000.

Ackroyd, Peter. *Shakespeare. The Biography*. London: Vintage, 2006.

Ackroyd, Peter. *Thames, Sacred River*. London: Chatto & Windus, 2007.

Bede's Ecclesiastical History of England. A Revised Translation by A. M. Sellar, London, 1907. Project Gutenberg edition

Bryne, T. *Local Government in Britain*. London: Penguin, 1994.

Bryson, Bill. *Shakespeare. The World as a Stage*. London: Harper Perennial, 2007.

Burton, Anthony. *Hadrian's Wall Path*. London: Aurum, 2004.

Caesar, Gaius Iulius. *De Bello Gallico & Other Commentaries of Julius Caesar*, translated by W.A. MacDevitt. Everman's Library, 1915. Project Gutenberg online edition.

Cannon, John/Anne Hargreaves (eds.). *Kings and Queens of Britain*. Oxford: OUP, 2001.

Churchill, Winston. *A History of the English-Speaking Peoples*. London: Cassell, 1956–1958.

Colquhoun, Kate. *Taste. The Story of Britain through its Cooking*. London: Bloomsbury, 2007.

Daeschner, J.R. *True Brits. A Tour of Twenty-First Century Britain in All Its Bog-Snorkelling, Gurning and Cheese-Rolling Glory*. London: Arrow, 2004.

Domesday Book. http.//www.nationalarchives.gov.uk/domesday/

Engels, Friedrich. *The Condition of the Working Classes in England in 1844*. London, 1892. Project Gutenberg Online Edition

Ferguson, Niall. *Empire. How Britain Made the Modern World*. London: Penguin, 2003.

Fox, Kate. *Watching the English. The Hidden Rules of English Behaviour*. London: Hodder & Stoughton, 2004.

Foyle, Christopher. *Foyle's Philavery. A Treasury of Unusual Words*. Edinburgh: Chambers, 2007.

Frere, Sheppard. *Britannia. A History of Roman Britain*. London: Pimlico, 1987.

Fry, Fred. *Patterns of Power. The Military Campaigns of Alfred the Great*. Ely: Melrose, 2006.

Green, Judith A. *The Aristocracy of Norman England*. Cambridge: CUP, 1997.

Hallett, Mark/Christine Riding. *Hogarth*. London: Tate, 2006.

Harper-Bill, Christopher/Elisabeth van Houts (eds.).
    A Companion to the Anglo-Norman World. Ipswich:
    Boydell, 2003.

Her Majesty's Stationery Office. *Aspects of Britain. Local
    Government*. London, 1996.

Hochschild, Adam. *Bury the Chains. Prophets and Rebels
    in the Fight to Free an Empire's Slaves*. Boston: Mariner,
    2006.

Houts, Elisabeth van (Ed.). *The Normans in Europe*.
    Manchester: MUP, 2000.

Hutton, Ronald. *The Stations of the Sun. A History of the
    Ritual Year in Britain*. Oxford: Oxford Paperbacks, 1997.

James, C.L.R. *Letters from London* [1932]. Oxford: Signal,
    2003.

Kermode, Frank. *The Age of Shakespeare*. London:
    Weidenfeld & Nicholson, 2004.

Kingsnorth, Paul. *Real England. The Battle Against the
    Bland*. London: Portobello, 2008.

Le Vay, Benedict. *Eccentric Britain. The Bradt Guide to
    Britain's Follies and Foibles*. Chalfont St. Peter: Bradt,
    2005.

Maconie, Stuart. *Adventures on the High Teas. In Search of
    Middle England*. London: Ebury, 2009.

Marr, Andrew. *A History of Modern Britain*. London: Pan,
    2007.

Miall, Antony/David Milsted. *Xenophobe's Guide to the
    English*. London: Oval, 1993.

Mikes, George. *How to be a Brit. A George Mikes Minibus.* London: Penguin, 1984.

Moody, Paul/Robin Turner. *The Rough Pub Guide. A Celebration of the Great British Boozer.* London: Orion, 2008.

O'Farrell, John. *An Utterly Impartial History of Britain, or. 2000 Years of Upper Class Idiots in Charge.* London: Black Swan, 2007.

Oxford Dictionary of National Biography. www.oxforddnb. com

Paxman, Jeremy. *The English. A Portrait of a People.* London: Penguin, 1998.

Paxman, Jeremy. *On Royalty.* London: Penguin, 2006.

Paxman, Jeremy. *The Victorians. Britain Through the Paintings of the Age.* London: BBC Books, 2009.

Pryor, Francis. *Britain AD. A Quest for England, Arthur, and the Anglo-Saxons.* London: Harper Collins, 2004.

Rennison, Nick. *The Book of Lists: London.* Edinburgh: Canongate, 2006.

Roud, Steve. *The English Year. A Month-by-Month Guide to the Nation's Customs and Festivals, from May Day to Mischief Night.* London: Penguin, 2006.

Royle, Trevor. *The British Civil War. The Wars of the Three Kingdoms, 1638–1660.* New York: Palgrave Macmillan, 2004.

Sitwell, Edith. *English Eccentrics* [1933]. London: Penguin, 1971.

Slater, Nigel. *Eating for England. The Delights and Eccentricities of the British at Table*. London: Harper Perennial, 2007.

Smit, Tim. *Eden*. London: Transworld, 2001.

Tyack, Geoffrey, *Blue Guide. Oxford and Cambridge*. New York: A & C Black, 2004.

Tickletooth, Tabitha. *The Dinner Question; or: How to Dine Well & Economically*. [1860] Facsimile. Totnes: Prospect, 1999.

Ward, Benedicta. *The Venerable Bede*. London: Continuum, 1998.

Weightman, Gavin. *The Industrial Revolutionaries. The Creators of the Modern World 1776–1914*. London: Atlantic, 2007.

Index